CAMBRIDGE LIBRARY COLLECTION

Books of enduring scholarly value

History

The books reissued in this series include accounts of historical events and movements by eye-witnesses and contemporaries, as well as landmark studies that assembled significant source materials or developed new historiographical methods. The series includes work in social, political and military history on a wide range of periods and regions, giving modern scholars ready access to influential publications of the past.

Naval and Military Essays

As Europe was poised on the cusp of the Great War (1914–1918), issues of national defence were of paramount concern. Despite the importance to German security of concentrating its resources on continental defence within Europe, the preceding years had been steeped in the cult of the navy. Germany's daunting pursuit of Weltpolitik had raised a serious challenge to traditional British naval hegemony. At issue were the future course of international relations, economic development and – crucially – the balance of power on both regional and global scales. Published in early 1914, some papers in this volume reviewed historic contributions of the British navy, offering a timely opportunity to formulate a better understanding of how the navy might be expected to perform in the future. The contents are evenly divided between essays on naval and military history, with the value of such historical analyses to contemporary officers being an explicit theme throughout.

Cambridge University Press has long been a pioneer in the reissuing of out-of-print titles from its own backlist, producing digital reprints of books that are still sought after by scholars and students but could not be reprinted economically using traditional technology. The Cambridge Library Collection extends this activity to a wider range of books which are still of importance to researchers and professionals, either for the source material they contain, or as landmarks in the history of their academic discipline.

Drawing from the world-renowned collections in the Cambridge University Library, and guided by the advice of experts in each subject area, Cambridge University Press is using state-of-the-art scanning machines in its own Printing House to capture the content of each book selected for inclusion. The files are processed to give a consistently clear, crisp image, and the books finished to the high quality standard for which the Press is recognised around the world. The latest print-on-demand technology ensures that the books will remain available indefinitely, and that orders for single or multiple copies can quickly be supplied.

The Cambridge Library Collection will bring back to life books of enduring scholarly value across a wide range of disciplines in the humanities and social sciences and in science and technology.

Naval and Military Essays

*Being Papers Read in the Naval and Military
Section at the International Congress of
Historical Studies, 1913*

JULIAN STAFFORD CORBETT

CAMBRIDGE UNIVERSITY PRESS

Cambridge New York Melbourne Madrid Cape Town Singapore São Paolo Delhi

Published in the United States of America by Cambridge University Press, New York

www.cambridge.org
Information on this title: www.cambridge.org/9781108003490

This edition first published 1914
This digitally printed version 2009

ISBN 978-1-108-00349-0

CAMBRIDGE NAVAL AND MILITARY SERIES

General Editors—JULIAN S. CORBETT, LL.M., F.S.A.
H. J. EDWARDS, C.B., M.A.

NAVAL AND MILITARY ESSAYS

CAMBRIDGE UNIVERSITY PRESS
London: FETTER LANE, E.C.
C. F. CLAY, Manager

Edinburgh: 100 PRINCES STREET
Berlin: A. ASHER AND CO.
Leipzig: F. A. BROCKHAUS
New York: G. P. PUTNAM'S SONS
Bombay and Calcutta: MACMILLAN AND CO., Ltd.
Toronto: J. M. DENT & SONS, Ltd.
Tokyo: THE MARUZEN-KABUSHIKI-KAISHA

NAVAL AND MILITARY ESSAYS

BEING PAPERS READ
IN THE
NAVAL AND MILITARY SECTION
AT THE
INTERNATIONAL
CONGRESS OF HISTORICAL STUDIES
1913

Cambridge:
at the University Press
1914

PREFACE

AFTER the conclusion of the International Congress of Historical Studies in April last, in the scheme of which a Naval and Military Section was included for the first time, it seemed desirable to some members of the Committee in charge of the new Section that the papers read should be published in book form. The authorities of the Congress having decided in due course that they were unable themselves to make provision for such publication, it was suggested that the papers in question might appropriately be collected to form a volume in the Naval and Military Series which had recently been announced by the Cambridge University Press. The suggestion was readily accepted by the Editors of the Series and the Syndics of the Press.

The present volume contains, in full text or in summary (where, for one reason or another, the full text was not obtainable), the papers on Naval and Military subjects read at the Congress. The full text of Sir John Laughton's paper appeared in the July number of *The Cornhill Magazine*; that of Dr Holland Rose's paper in the October number of *The Edinburgh Review*; and Mr

Atkinson's paper, of which a summary is here given, formed the subject of a lecture delivered by him at the Royal United Service Institution on 29th October last. The Editors of the Series desire to express their grateful thanks to all the authors for their courtesy in contributing their manuscript, or in compiling summaries, for the present volume; to Sir A. W. Ward, Master of Peterhouse, and Lieut.-Colonel F. B. Maurice, for valued help in connection with the Military Essays; and to the Publishers of the two periodicals above-mentioned in the case of the papers concerned.

The index of proper names has been made by Miss M. H. James.

JULIAN S. CORBETT
H. J. EDWARDS

31 *January*, 1914

CONTENTS

A—NAVAL

B—MILITARY

NAVAL ESSAYS

A

HISTORIANS AND NAVAL HISTORY [1]

BY SIR JOHN K. LAUGHTON

THE Navy has had such an important influence
on the development of England's national life
that it may well cause some surprise to find that
our people in general know so little of our Naval
History, and still more, perhaps, to find that as
a rule, until within the last forty or fifty years,
our historians paid little attention to it. The
notices they give of naval movements are quite
perfunctory, relate only to those which come more
distinctly into open view, and are chiefly remarkable for extreme misapprehension. I am not
referring merely to the ordinary textbooks, though
—as far as they are concerned—England might
be in the geographical position of Bohemia, and
it is from them that our young people get their
first, and, in too many cases, also their last impressions. In their way, the greater historians
are almost equally bad. The least so, in this
respect, is Lord Stanhope (Mahon), who in his
History of the Eighteenth Century—a period more
than usually important in our naval history—
does mention the chief patent facts, and, by

[1] By kind permission of the Editor of *The Cornhill Magazine*.

3

avoiding details, avoids also gross blunders. But he had no knowledge of facts that were not patent. He did not know, for instance, the very important share that the Navy had in the failure of the Rebellion of 1745; and when he does go into detail, as in his account of the relief of Barcelona in 1706, he blunders egregiously, by trusting to a spurious journal, into the authenticity of which he had not examined.

Of all earlier writers, Macaulay is perhaps the worst, for detail was Macaulay's speciality. This leads him often into error, and when he talks of naval affairs, he is perhaps more than usually incongruous and inaccurate. I have no doubt that his intentions were good, but his performance was very bad. And the scale of his naval notices, no less than their matter, seems to show that he but lightly esteemed them in comparison with the weighty affairs of *terra firma*. He allots, for instance, four pages to the account of the battle of La Hogue—" the first great victory," he says, " that the English had gained over the French since the day of Agincourt "; a victory which Ranke has spoken of as giving the command of the sea to the English. Whether either of these is a true estimate, I do not stop to inquire ; the point I wish to make is, that with an inordinate amount of irrelevant and quite unauthenticated padding, he tells the story in four pages, of which something like every other line contains a grotesque blunder ; but to Steinkirk, a battle more Dutch than English, and now perhaps best known by the necktie that was named from it, he devotes six pages ; and to Landen, also a Dutch battle and known to modern readers mainly by Macaulay's own magnificent narrative —into the entire accuracy of which I am not called on to examine—he gives nine ; and this, though neither of them affected in any important degree the course or the result of the war.   They only happened to be fought on land.

In other passages where he refers to naval transactions, he seems to be guided either by spite and political prejudice, or by pamphleteers who wrote under similar guidance.   People are apt to think that they do know something of the naval history of this particular war,[1] because Macaulay had the supreme art of making himself read.   They really know very little about it, because in their study of it they are following a blind leader of the blind.

If, in other periods of our history, other historians have made fewer blunders, it is that they have tried to avoid speaking of naval affairs at all.   When they have not been able to do that, they have spoken of the Navy as a mere engine for fighting battles and sometimes for winning victories, glorious, but of no great consequence. Of the more certain and unceasing work of the

[1] War of the League of Augsburg, 1689-1697.

Navy, the constant, grinding pressure which it brings on our enemies, few really understand anything. Only a few years ago, the Council of the Naval Exhibition at Chelsea (1891), a Council, largely consisting of naval officers of high rank, decided that they could not put forward prominently the preamble of the old Act of Parliament, commonly known as the Articles of War, because it would seem a piece of vulgar braggadocio. The words objected to were that it is the Navy " on which, under the Good Providence of God, the wealth, safety and strength of the kingdom chiefly depend." This Council, that is to say, had no understanding of any work of the Navy except its fighting battles ; no real understanding of the work which many of them had spent their lives in doing ; no understanding of the work done by the Navy during the ten years of the Napoleonic War after Trafalgar, when there were no battles at all.

And so, only to an exaggerated extent, it is with modern readers over the whole course of our history ; where there are no battles, there is no naval history. A modern writer, happily still living, has said that when England entered on the War of the Spanish Succession, she was A naval power ; when she emerged from it, she was THE naval power. Does the ordinary reader ask himself how this was ? He reads of only one battle and that not a decisive victory ; he reads

—if he has an inquiring mind—of many skirmishes and several single-ship fights, in which victory did not always fall to the English ; he reads that the French were capturing our merchant ships and even our men-of-war, on our own coasts, as a whale captures herrings. At no time have the achievements of French ships shone with greater *éclat.* It was the age of Cassard, of Forbin, of Du Guay Trouin—names which may be placed in juxtaposition with the most brilliant in English history ; men over whom our ships and fleets won no advantage. And yet, *Respice finem !* At the end of the war, England was THE naval power. Is it braggadocio to say that ? Fortunately for us, it was a foreigner—a student[1] of naval history in its widest sense—who made the statement. It remains for our historians to explain it.

Again, it is, I think, familiarly known that in the Civil War of the seventeenth century, the Navy adhered to the Parliament, but as no battles were fought, the advantage to the Parliament was believed to be trifling, if not negligible. It was left for Dr Gardiner, after more than two hundred years, to show that it was really the determining factor of the struggle ; but even Gardiner did not consider it necessary to examine why the Navy took the Parliamentary side. Still less has any historian thought it necessary to dwell on the Navy as, to a considerable extent,

[1] Admiral Mahan, U.S.N.

a cause of the triumph of the Yorkists in the Wars of the Roses ; or, going back to still earlier days, of the triumph of the Barons over Henry III.

The fact is that, till quite recently, historians have considered naval history as outside their purview ; separated from political history, from ecclesiastical, social, industrial, commercial, even military history, as by a series of watertight bulk-heads ; having no earthly connection with them and only to be spoken of when a dramatic situation—Hawke, for instance, at Quiberon Bay, Nelson at Copenhagen—promised to be effective. They have, therefore, not studied the general action of the Navy and have known nothing of it. They have left everything relating to naval affairs to a class of writers who have been spoken of as " Naval Historians "—sometimes, it would almost seem, in analogy with the name of the Guinea-Pig.[1]

The early chroniclers knew no such division of labour ; they wrote what they saw, what they heard and what they imagined ; and about naval affairs with the same freedom and the same ignorance as about everything else. The scraps relating to naval history have to be picked out piecemeal and put together as the student best can. The absurdities have to be passed over, or explained away when they are too palpable. One

[1] There are possibly some people who do not know that the little animal is so called because he is not a pig, and does not come from Guinea.

that has always struck me as peculiarly delightful, as illustrating the chroniclers' refusal to be restrained by the trammels of natural science— astronomy say, and geography—is Froissart's statement that at Sluys, the English worked or rowed to the north-east all the forenoon, so that they might charge down on the French line with the advantage of the sun. We accept the statement that the English did make the reported movement ; it was a thing that could be seen, and no doubt was seen by thousands ; but to suppose that they made it in order that they might have the sun in the faces of their fighting men as they charged to the south, is to suppose them imbecile. Why they made it may well be a subject for discussion ; but whatever the advantage they sought, they paid a heavy price for it.

It was not till the seventeenth century that men began writing on naval history as a thing apart, and then very much as chroniclers of their own experiences. Such, at least, is Sir William Monson, who seems to have always kept in view the idea that his first duty was to represent his own conduct in the most favourable light. His writings are useful, suggestive, and often amusing ; but in reading them it is necessary to keep in mind that the notes from which he wrote were very defective, his memory imperfect, and his bias pronounced. After him I must refer to

John Evelyn, a man who was, in civil affairs, frequently connected with the Navy, and an intimate associate of Samuel Pepys. He is said to have written a history of the Second Dutch War, and to have sent his manuscript to Pepys for amendment or criticism ; between the two the MS. was lost, and—less fortunate than Carlyle's *French Revolution*—was not rewritten. If the story is true, it is possible that the MS. may yet be found ; but there is absolutely no evidence that it was ever written, and I, myself, am disposed to think that it was not. That Evelyn had the intention of writing it, I know. Some time since, while doing some work in the Record Office, I came, quite by accident, on a sheet with the well-known signature of J. E., endorsed —" Queries for Mr Williamson ; to be communicated to my Lord Arlington." [1] The queries, though unanswered, are themselves very interesting, and seem to show more than the average seventeenth-century writer's estimate of a historian's duty, *e.g.* :—

1. The rise of the quarrel and how to justify C. Holmes' action at Guinea ?

7. The Dutch action at Sheerness and Chatham and upon whom the miscarriage and our losses are to be charged ?

8. Concerning the treaty, by whom first sought ?

[1] F. O. Holland, ccliv. 290.

How managed ? Why Breda was preferred to London ?

And as additional :—

1. What is to be said of the French King's declaring for the Hollander, and his pronouncing US the aggressors ?

5. The action at Bergen and Negotiation with the King of Denmark.

7. Why the fleet was divided and by whose advice—to vindicate my Lord Arlington in point of intelligence ?

9. Why His Majesty parted with Dunkirk to the French, so near the rupture with the Hollander ?

We can, I am afraid, quite well understand why there are no answers to these questions ; and we may wonder what use Evelyn would have made of the answers, true or false, if he had got any ; but that he felt the historian's curiosity on the several points he raised must stand to his credit.

It would seem that Josiah Burchett ought to be classed as a " Naval Historian," for his book—a folio of near 800 pages—bears the high-sounding title : *A complete History of the most remarkable Transactions at Sea, from the earliest accounts of time to the conclusion of the last*

war with France, etc. etc.   In reality, the only part
of it that has any value is the part that relates
to his own time.   As a boy, he entered the service
of the Admiralty as Pepys' servant and clerk ;
and as a young man, after the Revolution obtained
employment as Russell's secretary.   In 1695,
being then about thirty, he was appointed joint
secretary of the Admiralty ; and sole secretary
in 1698.   So he continued till a few years before
his death in 1746, at the age of eighty or there-
abouts.   In 1720, when he published the *Transactions at Sea*, he had been twenty-five years
secretary of the Admiralty, and four or five
years more secretary to the commander-in-chief
in the Channel and in the Mediterranean.   He
had intimate knowledge of everything that was
done or had been proposed during the wars of
William III. and Anne.   But he had no experience
as an author, nor—apparently—any natural gift.
His partiality for Russell is not prominently put
forward, but we ought not to forget that it is
there ; he omits altogether or slurs over many
minor transactions and especially when they
might be thought distasteful to the English ; and
he writes, at all times, with the official reticence
of the secretary's office.   There is no doubt that
he might have explained many points which
remain mysterious, or as to which we have to seek
enlightenment in the French Memoirs of the
time—of Du Guay Trouin, of Forbin, or—most

delightful and most inaccurate of all—of Jean Doublet.[1]

Thomas Corbett, who was secretary to Sir George Byng in the Mediterranean, and was afterwards at the Admiralty, first as assistant and then as successor to Burchett, was the author of a neat little book on *The Expedition to Sicily*, which is fairly trustworthy and has the great merit of being concise. And after him, we come to Thomas Lediard, the first of " Naval Historians," both in time and merit. Lediard was an attaché of the Embassy at Hamburg, and was for several years lent to the Duke of Marlborough as foreign secretary. He must have been a good linguist, and wrote the history of the reigns of William III. and Anne, besides a Life of the Duke of Marlborough ; and in 1735 brought out *The Naval History of England . . . from the Norman Conquest . . . to the conclusion of* 1734. By his intercourse with Marlborough, he necessarily knew something of the practical conditions of war ; he had made voyages by sea—if only the crossing over to Hamburg, and at any rate could talk of a ship without mixing the bowsprit and the rudder, or of a fleet, without telling how the Admiral rode up to the head of it.[2] His book does really show some research, and though very

---

[1] These Memoirs—of Du Guay Trouin more especially—are much more trustworthy than might be supposed from their lively and perhaps self-conscious style.

[2] A well-known *Life of Blake* has described him as doing this.

far from being up to the modern standard, is—
for his age—a very honest piece of work. The
early period is scanty and not too accurate. That
is his misfortune rather than his fault ; and for
the rest he draws freely, but not blindly, on
Burchett, who is, of course, the foundation of all
later works.

Dr John Campbell in 1742, 1745, published
the celebrated *Lives of the Admirals*, which,
owing largely, I believe, to its convenient size—
in 8vo—took a high place in popular favour from
the first ; it has often been republished, with
additional volumes by other and much inferior
writers. Campbell did not know much about
the Navy, but he was an industrious student of
history, ancient and modern, and his work abounds
in deductions and suggestions, some of which are
extremely interesting, though many, based on a
very imperfect knowledge of the facts, seem now
principally remarkable for their wildness.

The warlike attitude of Europe in 1755 appears
to have suggested to the booksellers or book-
makers—it is impossible to say which—that a
new Naval History might command the market,
and the possible demand was grabbed at by a
certain John Hill—an apothecary and quack
doctor, a man described by Dr Johnson as want-
ing in veracity, and, in the *Dictionary of
National Biography*, as of unscrupulous character and unlimited impudence—who brought

out *Naval History of Britain . . . to the conclusion of the year* 1756. It professes to be compiled from the papers of Captain George Berkeley, whose name he did not know how to spell. Captain Berkeley died in 1746, and there is not the least probability that he had any papers of consequence, or that Hill knew anything of him ; though it is possible that he bought or otherwise got possession of Berkeley's copy of Lediard, which may have had some manuscript notes. It is perhaps more probable that he merely fixed on Berkeley as a high-sounding name.

Not altogether different, but of a more respectable character is the work of John Entick, who, though he had no familiarity with the Navy, was a man of considerable and varied attainments. A schoolmaster, possibly a clergyman, author of several historical and religious books, not to mention a Ready Reckoner and a Latin Dictionary, he published in 1757 the *New Naval History*, mainly a transcript of Lediard, but swollen to an inordinate degree by the insertion of irrelevant matter. The feature in it that most attracts me is the economical problem of its production. It is a folio of the largest size, of nearly 900 pages, of small type, containing roughly 1500 thousand words. By comparison with the dates of his other books, which are very many, he must have planned this, arranged it—of course there is no research—composed his own matter, which is sometimes quite sensible, written it out, or scissored and pasted it, and passed it through the press within a year. Those who have any experience in the production of books will be able to formulate the problem more exactly. The bulk is approximately that of the ten volumes of Gardiner's *History of England*, 1603-1642, the work of nearly twenty years. But Gardiner's principle, as laid down by himself, was " that it was the duty of a serious inquirer to search into the original causes of great events, rather than, for the sake of catching at an audience, to rush unprepared upon the great events themselves." It is unnecessary to define the principle on which Entick acted. In 1763 he published, in four volumes 8vo, *A History of the Late (Seven Years) War*, a crude compilation of such reports, official or non-official, as were accessible. It is a convenient and not very untrustworthy record of simple facts, without any further value. Certainly not one that ought to be cited as an authority.

Another and not more particularly trashy compilation put abroad in 1779, in five volumes 8vo, by John Payne, a bookseller whom misfortune turned into " an indefatigable manufacturer of books," owed a certain vogue which it long had to its more convenient format, and partly perhaps to its being published as by George

Augustus Hervey, a pseudonym no doubt meant to convey the idea of Augustus John Hervey, Earl of Bristol, whose name was then well before the public both as admiral, and as husband of Elizabeth Chudleigh. There are others, anonymous or pseudonymous, some of which I have seen, but about which I have no notes. They appeared to me quite worthless. But of all these so-called " Naval Historians " of the eighteenth century, from Lediard to Payne, the works, though describing the evident facts in varying degrees of merit or demerit, are not histories at all, if by HISTORY we are to understand something more than the mere relation of bare facts, without any examination into causes, any explanation of results. Of the causes or aims of wars, of the controlling policy, of the strategy or of the tactics, they are ignorant or worse than ignorant.

The century ends with two men of a widely different character, whom I prefer to speak of, not by the discredited title, but as writers on naval biography and history. In 1794-8, John Charnock brought out his *Biographia Navalis*, in six volumes 8vo, being the lives of all naval officers of post rank between 1660 and 1760, with some of a few years later. Charnock was a man of some education, had some service in the Navy, though it is not clear in what capacity, and was, in later life, a familiar friend and neighbour of

B

Captain William Locker,[1] who had made himself
a storehouse of naval tradition and anecdote.
It may perhaps be said that the *Biographia
Navalis* derives its principal value from Locker
and documents which Locker had collected.   It
is interesting and useful, but calls for caution.

A more important work—perhaps the most
important work of the century—is Robert
Beatson's *Naval and Military Memoirs of Great
Britain from* 1727 *to* 1783.   As a young man,
Beatson was an officer of engineers, served in
the futile expedition against Rochéfort in 1757
and in the West Indies during the continuance
of the war.   After the peace of 1763 he was put
on half-pay and seems to have spent the rest of
his life in or near Aberdeen, occupying himself
partly with scientific farming and partly with
literary pursuits.   His *Political Index* is a
useful work, which, in the modernised form of
Haydn's *Book of Dignities*, still keeps the field.
The *Naval and Military Memoirs* (1790-1804)
is military only so far as the two services were
acting together.   The main purport of the book
is naval, is based on the best evidence then obtainable, abounds in detail and in careful, judicious
criticism, and is, altogether, very far superior to
anything that had then been published.   It is
nowhere explicitly stated, but there is good reason

---

[1] Locker was Lieutenant-Governor of Greenwich Hospital;
Charnock was living at Blackheath.

to believe that Admiral Philip Patton was, to some extent at least, a collaborator in the work.[1]

The opening of the nineteenth century brings us to the great French War, and for several years the men who wrote on naval history confined themselves to the story of their own time. The *Naval Chronicle*, edited by James S. Clarke, a naval chaplain, and John McArthur, purser and secretary, best known perhaps by their *Life of Nelson*, is simply, what its name says, a chronicle, and as such is a very fair authority. When it makes excursions into the story of the past, it is not to be trusted. It was published monthly during the war, and extends to 40 six-monthly volumes 8vo, badly printed on bad paper.

A far more important work is *The Naval History of Great Britain, from the declaration of war by France in 1793 to the accession of George IV.*, by William James, 5 vols. 8vo, 1822-4. In writing this, James had access to much written and personal evidence of the most direct kind, and the result was a work of extraordinary merit, within its limits. It avoids, with marked purpose, anything relating to national history, strategy or the bearing of events, which the author was, apparently, unable to understand. It is conceited, dogmatic and prejudiced to an extreme degree, so as to deprive its judgments of all title to respect ; but it was described by an

[1] *Letters of Lord Barham*, ii. 384.

early reviewer, as approaching " as nearly to
perfection, in its own line, as any historical work
ever did." [1]   The criticism has done a great deal
of harm ; for students finding that this perfect
book could not be read, concluded that this was
the fault of the subject, not of the presentation of
it ; and that naval history was not for them.
There is no doubt that it cannot be read con-
tinuously ; but it is invaluable as a book of
reference, and still more so since the recent
publication of a detailed Index.[2]

Edward P. Brenton, a captain in the Navy
and a follower of Lord St Vincent, whose Life he
wrote, was also the author of a *Naval History
of Great Britain from* 1783 *to* 1822 (1823, 5 vols.
8vo ; 2nd edition in 2 vols.), a book of a remark-
ably good plan but of very feeble execution.
The narrative is, everywhere, of what the author,
with no idea of sifting evidence or discriminating
between truth and falsehood, thought might or
ought to have taken place rather than of what
did.   As a psychological study of the Brenton
type of mind, it is interesting, but as a history
of the War is almost worthless.   John Marshall's
Royal Naval Biography (12 vols. 8vo, 1823-
1835) is a record of the lives of every then living
naval officer of and above commander's rank,

[1] *Edinburgh Review*, lxxi. 121.
[2] By the Navy Records Society ; its references are to the
stereotyped edition in 6 vols. cr. 8vo.

written, in the main, from information supplied by the subjects themselves, and is thus a first hand authority; but its statements must, of course, be carefully weighed in the same way as all autobiographical statements.

The last writer I have occasion to mention is Sir Nicholas Harris Nicolas, a lieutenant in the Navy, who on his retirement, became a zealous student of history, wrote several standard books, whose merit has been very generally recognised, and began a *History of the Royal Navy from the earliest times to the wars of the French Revolution.* The first two volumes, published in 1847, come down to the wars of Henry V., but death prevented the continuation, which would possibly have been equally prevented by lack of financial support. The book is more a history of the Navy than a naval history; in neither respect is it exhaustive; probably the evidence was not then accessible; for even now there is much—very much—that has not been examined; but as it is, and as far as it goes, it is incomparably the best naval history that we have. It must serve as a foundation for future writers; but it is not easy reading.

What these future writers are doing or going to do, I am not able to say. I am now on the retired list, and read little but novels. But from these, I permit myself to derive hope and encouragement. A short time ago I read in one

to the effect that Nature (under direction) supplies meat and vegetables ; that Art (also under
direction) supplies cooks ; when the two join
hands, you get an enjoyable dinner. So it is
with all history, naval history as well as all other.
Nature supplies records and other original material ;
Art, directed by study and practice, supplies
literary skill, and a knowledge that people now-
adays will not read a book which they cannot
hold in their hands while sitting in an easy chair.
When we have the two properly united, we shall
have a naval history which, like good wine, will
need no bush, and will wipe away the stain of
ignorance from our countrymen. When they
really know and understand what the Navy has
done in time past, they will be able to understand what the Navy may be trusted to do in the
future, and will have gone far on the way to
understanding the problem of national defence.

STAFF HISTORIES

BY JULIAN CORBETT

Of late years there has been a large output of
work from the Historical Sections of Naval and
Military Staffs, which has wrought a revolution
in the study of war history. No historian
whose task has brought him in touch with this
work can fail to appreciate its value, nor in
the care and thoroughness of its methods can
we fail to recognise a complete change in the
attitude of the Services to history. The underlying cause of the change is not far to seek.
It is, primarily at least, due to the sound and
philosophical method which the Historical
Sections have adopted that has led them
directly to an appreciation of the practical living
value of history—that has revealed history
not as a museum of antiquities, but as a treasure-
house of rich experience.

For I would venture to say that the scepticism
as to the practical value of historical study
which formerly existed in the Services—and especially in the Naval Service—was mainly due to
unsound method. The common procedure was
that men, who from their own practical experience

had convinced themselves that some particular method or means of conducting war should be adopted, were accustomed to go to such history as was available for facts to demonstrate their preconceived opinion. Their opponents met them with a similar selection of facts, and the inevitable result was a sceptical feeling that history like statistics could prove anything, and with practical men history was brought into contempt. That has now passed away, under the influence of more philosophical methods, and officers no longer look upon history as a kind of dust heap from which a convenient brick may be extracted to hurl at their opponents. They no longer go to it to prove some empirical view of tactics or material, or to show that some battle or other was fought in the way they think it ought to have been fought. They go to it as a mine of experience where alone the gold is to be found, from which right doctrine—the soul of warfare— can be built up.

If we were to reduce the change that has taken place to a rough generalisation we might say—that formerly men went to history to prove they were right; now they go to it to find out where they are wrong ; or, as it has been well said, they go to history to search for principles, not to prove those which they believe they have already found.

The main question then with regard to Staff

Histories is no longer concerned with their value or purpose ; it is concerned rather with the best means of producing them, the best means, that is, of getting from them the desired results. And in endeavouring to find a solution we have first to face the fact that these histories are not all in the same category.

A broad distinction will at once suggest itself between histories of bygone wars, waged with material that is now quite obsolete and under conditions that no longer exist, from which we can only derive the broader doctrines ; and histories that deal with the wars of yesterday, in which, in spite of the rapid development of material, we seek for closer and more direct light on the wars of to-morrow.

Each class has its own special value and its own facilities of production. As an example of the first class we may take the German Staff History of the Seven Years' War. That shows us at once that the distant standpoint, from which the war is regarded, permits a seizure of its salient features. Unimportant detail disappears and a broad treatment is possible which seems to bring out in bold touches the general principles which are inseparable from the conduct of all wars. From the distant standpoint we are also able to appreciate clearly the deflections of purely military operations which were caused by political exigencies and influences, and to which modern military theory attaches so much importance. For in the case of the older wars there is no longer any reason why such matters should be kept secret. On this point, it is true, this particular history is not quite satisfactory, since it is confined to the continental and European theatre of the war, and the influence of the maritime theatre is ignored.

For the history of the older wars we have also another type of work—a good example of which is Colonel Desbrière's *Projets et tentatives de débarquement aux Iles Brittanniques*, 1798-1805, issued under direction of the French General Staff. Here is a work that aims not so much at a history of a particular war as at the solution of a certain war problem; and to do this it proceeds on lines opposite to the type of the German History. So far from seeking mainly by the broad treatment to detach general principles, it offers a complete collection of documents, orders, and statistics from which the solution of the problem may be extracted by close study. But the lucid comment is interwoven which leaves us in little doubt what the correct answer is.

So successful indeed is that work that it seems to point strongly to what is the right use for Historical Sections to make of the older history. It suggests that Historical Sections should not concern themselves with producing regular histories of such wars, but rather should go to them for the solution of special problems—so that the whole experience at our command may be brought to bear on the solution we are seeking.

An additional argument for taking this view is that, for reasons which will be suggested later, it is probable that the production of regular histories of the older wars is more within the province and capacity of civilian historians and may with advantage be left to them.

These considerations, however, do not apply with anything like the same strength to our second category—that is, histories which are required as soon as possible after a war has been fought, such as our own history of the Boer War and the Russian history of the Russo-Japanese War. These necessarily demand the study of the particular war as a whole ; for their conspicuous merit is that their object is avowedly to study the mistakes that were made with a view to preventing their recurrence. This leads to an illuminating frankness which is the marrow of real history.

But they labour under two drawbacks. One is, that frankness about political and other external deflections is not entirely possible, since the time has not come when such matters can be laid openly upon the table. The other, that since they are written in the lifetime of the men who fought them there is a tendency to modify criticism. In close connection with this there is a feeling

that the history must not only be a Staff History
—in the higher sense of an instructional work—
but it must also serve as a complete chronicle of
the war, in which the part of every unit must
have justice done to it, with the result that
we are sometimes smothered with a mass of
detail acquired at vast labour and expense which
has little or no value for the main purpose in
hand.

I am not suggesting that these defects can be
entirely avoided. Probably time alone can provide the complete remedy. Still it must be said
that in the eyes of a professed historian these
works are not quite histories, but rather they are—
like collections of documents—materials for history.
And I trust that I may be pardoned for saying
that probably an expert historian—proceeding
on the well-known principles of his craft—would
indicate ways in which some of these defects
could be avoided and by which the book might
be rendered much more digestible to a hard-
worked officer seeking to improve his knowledge
of his profession.

I make this comment with the less diffidence
because it is possible to point to an example
where the principles I refer to have been followed
by an officer who was also a man of letters and
an accomplished historian. I mean the official
history of the Tel-el-Kebir campaign by the late
General Sir Frederick Maurice. The whole affair

is dealt with by him in about 100 pages, and I believe it is held to be a very satisfactory and comprehensive account. True, the campaign was short and comparatively simple, but none the less I would submit we may look to this work as a standard of method to be approached as nearly as the subject in hand permits.

Further, I should like to make it clear that in drawing attention to the inordinate length and heaviness of recent Staff Histories we fully appreciate that these defects are the defects of their best qualities. They are due to the conscientious and minute research upon which the narratives are built up and the untiring efforts to be correct and just. They are defects with which every modern historian has to struggle in these days of voluminous material, but they can be overcome by a fuller study of the art of narrative and the art of selection. I do not pretend these things are easy; for usually they are the last qualities to which a professed historian attains after lifelong practice.

These considerations lead naturally to my second point—as to how Staff Histories can best be produced. Here, again, I would distinguish between considerations which apply generally and those which concern a British Staff.

Clearly, if Staff Histories are susceptible of the distinct classification I have indicated, the method of treatment is likely to vary, but in each case the crux seems to be co-operation. Take first the histories of the older wars. Here officers reaching back for their material find themselves on ground that is unfamiliar to them, but quite well known to professed historians. They have to set to work with a mass of purely historical evidence that requires special training for its right handling. The skill can be acquired, and I believe there are few better schools than a historical section, but it takes time, especially if the acquisition is attempted without expert instruction. And here, in justification of my suggestion that these histories are perhaps better left to professed historians, I would venture with deference to offer a few warnings which are addressed mainly to naval officers, partly because most of their history is so old and partly because it seems that military officers, from the nature of their education and the wealth and excellence of their literature, have a much better chance of acquiring the necessary skill and mental attitude, than the peculiar training and occupations of naval officers permit.

If, then, I may be allowed to do so—in no spirit of censure or superiority, but with a genuine desire to assist in the difficult path—I would say that for the unskilled hand endeavouring for himself to elucidate a problem by the experience of the long dead masters there are traps innumerable. Perhaps the best way to make the danger and difficulty clear is by analogy. In the mystery of the sea-craft there is something that sailors call "seamanship," an intangible but necessary equipment which they know it is extremely difficult for civilians to acquire. In its broader sense it is impossible to define or even to explain; but we know that it is something only to be mastered by long service afloat, and that it so completely permeates the whole subject of naval warfare that no civilian writers can hope to avoid grave error without the assistance of naval officers. Those of us at least who have dared to walk upon the waters know well the need of their helping hand.

On the other part, historians have something akin to it—something with which the training of a naval officer leaves him unfamiliar—and we call it "scholarship"; consequently he will sometimes devote his leisure to history with little suspicion that without some equipment in scholarship he will err as seriously as will civilians without seamanship. The one is as essential and as intangible as the other. Scholarship is only to be attained by long and devoted service —by long mental discipline, by regular initiation into the methods of dealing with historical evidence, of tracing it to its sources, of testing their value, and finally of raising upon it conclusions which are as free, as fallible human minds can make them, from preconceived ideas.

But in speaking of conclusions which are within the province of historical scholarship, it is important to make it clear that what is meant are historical and not technical conclusions. While emphatically repudiating any suggestion that the province of historians is merely to collect and marshal facts for officers to deal with, it is equally necessary to insist upon the line beyond which historians should not venture in drawing conclusions, and this line can be drawn very distinctly. It lies between historical conclusions, which depend upon the balance of historical evidence and disciplined historical judgment, and technical conclusions, which are arrived at by applying historical conclusions to the solution of modern technical problems. The first are clearly within the province of professed historians, the second are beyond their province and must be left to experts in the Services. The two spheres can easily be kept apart, and their mutual relations can at the same time be actively preserved, if it be only admitted that, as in naval matters, no technical conclusion is safe without seamanship, so no historical conclusion is safe without scholarship.

To clear the point with a concrete instance, it is submitted that the right type of battleship to-day is a technical conclusion. But on the other hand the determination of the principles which decided the type of battleship in the past

is an historical conclusion. With the type to-day
the historian has nothing to do, but it is his
business to see that false historical conclusions
are not used to prove that a particular modern
type is either right or wrong.

The practical outcome of these considerations
is that there are three ways in which naval history may be produced for staff purposes. The
ideal probably is free collaboration between the
historical expert and the naval expert. But
we may also look for it with confidence from the
naval officer who has been at the pains to acquire
the elements of historical technique either from
professed historians, or by practical work in an
Historical Section; and *vice versâ* from the
civilian who has had opportunity of learning the
lie of the more obvious pitfalls that beset the
path of the naval amateur, and who has taken
the trouble to master the not very extensive
professional literature which deals with the
principles of naval warfare.

It remains to inquire—what are the special
considerations which apply to the production of
Staff History in our own particular case? The
greater part of our peculiar war history is the
history of what Pitt called " maritime war "—that
is, war in which the Army and the Navy are
engaged together. This side of the subject has
received little attention from any staff and
consequently our experience is small. Till quite

c

recent years Historical Sections have had to deal
almost entirely with great continental wars, into
which the sea factor hardly entered, and consequently their history was dealt with naturally
by the military staffs and with excellent results.
But were we ever to try to deal with our own
war history in this way, it is obvious that serious
difficulty would arise. The most pronounced
deflections in war are those which naval operations exercise upon land operations and *vice versâ*.
So far, indeed, do these mutual reactions penetrate
a maritime war, when both Services are fully
engaged, that it becomes necessary to treat
Army and Navy as units of one combined force.
How, then, should the history of such wars be
produced? The answer seems obvious—by a joint-
Historical Section formed from both Services. The
question forced itself upon us some ten years ago,
when the struggle in the Far East confronted
us with a great war of the old and almost forgotten type. How was it to be dealt with?
Most countries, I believe, began to attack it with
two Historical Sections, the one naval and the
other military. We ourselves were among the
number, but as the preparation of the work
revealed how intimately the naval and military
operations were entwined it was decided to
amalgamate the two branches as one joint section
of the Committee of Defence under a single head.
It will be agreed that that was the logical

procedure, the method apparently best calculated to emphasise the essential unity of the land and sea forces of an island country and that it was an experiment that had to be tried. But whether the experiment has quite justified itself by success is not so clear. For all the excellent matter which the joint section is producing, for all the care and precision of its method, it leaves, so far as it has gone, an uneasy feeling that it has failed as a work of art. By failing as a work of art I mean it has failed in conveying the impression it set out to convey. Its outstanding characteristic is not a firm hold on the interaction of sea and land. It gives us not so much combined history as naval and military history in strata. We find naval operations arising out of a military situation or closely affecting it have to wait their time till the military narrative is completed, and by the time it is done we have lost the connecting thread. Again, the military narrative has to be broken in order to make room for naval operations that belong logically to a different stage of the general development, and we find with a sense of mental dislocation that we have been forming judgments without all the facts before us.

I would not exaggerate these defects, but any professed historian, practised in the art of marshalling complex narrative, can see that they are there and that they do detract from the value of an otherwise admirable book. What I wish to suggest is that these defects are in no way due to individuals, but that they are due to the system. It used to be thought, and the idea still lingers in continental staffs, that joint-expeditions should have a single commander-in-chief. The idea is logical—even obvious—one of those fallacies which are said to " stand to reason " ; but our experience proved it *was* a fallacy and that the only way to work such joint operations was with two co-equal commanders-in-chiefs acting in perfect and loyal harmony. With a single com-mander-in-chief, experience tells that the needs and limitations of one Service will too often be overridden by those of the other, and it is probable that an analogous process is inseparable from joint historical work.

But even if with a joint section a perfectly equal and smooth co-ordination could be obtained, we cannot escape another drawback. And that is this. The more thoroughly the work is done the more must it result in the student of each Service being harassed with a mass of detail which does not concern him and from which he can profit nothing.

What then is the solution ? I would submit that if the art of maritime warfare is to be clearly and profitably treated in historical exposition it must be done either from the sea or from the land. To deal adequately with a maritime war for staff purposes there must be two books and two Historical Sections. Each book, while preserving its own standpoint, must always keep in view the field of the other. It will deal in detail with the plans and operations of its own Service, but at the same time it will be careful to keep before the eyes of the reader the progress of the operations of the sister Service. They must never be dropped out of the narrative, and with a little of the technical skill which every historian has to exercise they may always be brought into view without obscuring or interrupting the main thread. They need only be given in outline, but they must be given or the true main thread will be lost. And this can be done without difficulty if the two sections work in intimate connection, each freely consulting the other in its special sphere, and each freely communicating to the other its special knowledge. In this way it would seem that the spirit of co-ordination, which means everything to a country like ours, may be fostered and its practical aspects studied far better than in one book. For each Service will be free to elaborate its own detail, and free to develop its own doctrine and at the same time be able to keep it in due subservience with that of the sister Service.

Nor need there be any practical difficulty in securing the necessary harmony of working. Recent experience goes to show that such harmony is readily obtained if both sections are under one roof—precisely as in our old conjunct expeditions it was obtained by both commanders-in-chief sailing in one ship.

That I venture to believe is the solution of the difficulty that has arisen—the difficulty which only experiment could have revealed, and that, I would submit, is the method upon which in the future our Staff History should proceed.

NAVAL HISTORY FROM THE NAVAL OFFICER'S POINT OF VIEW

BY CAPTAIN H. W. RICHMOND, R.N.

THE subject of my paper is one which has been dealt with before, and I make no pretence to new or original views. So long ago as 1874 Sir John Laughton gave an address in this theatre on the Scientific Study of Naval History, and again in 1896 he read another paper dealing with the same question. Whatever we have learnt of naval history in these recent years is due to him, and I should be sorry to read a paper on it without an acknowledgment of the deep indebtedness of the Navy to that distinguished historian.

I want to approach the subject of naval history from the point of view of its value to the naval officer. This may appear a narrow point of view, but I do not mean to say that I believe that the historian who makes this branch of history his particular study has only naval officers for his circle of readers; but it is as one of that circle that I venture to put my views, with a lingering apprehension that what the naval officer wants to get out of naval history is not really very different from what everybody else does. However, I can speak only of what I am acquainted with.

To the naval officer, naval history can be of great value, provided it is so treated that some practical end is served. Take it all round, we are a busy folk, and have only too little leisure for reading, and if we are going to read anything of a serious nature, we are inclined to wish that it shall increase our knowledge of our profession and be serviceable to us. Apart from the value of the study as a means of developing both general knowledge and the reasoning powers— and personally I attach the highest importance to both of these—it has other more obvious advantages. From it, and from it only, we learn how the naval forces of a country have been employed in war ; how they have exercised pressure on their own element, and enabled pressure to be exercised on the other element ; what limitations are set to the action of a naval force, and what results accrue from its action. We trace the varying phases of naval thought and see how certain phases have tended to produce certain results—and I know no place except in history where we can learn these things. Yet there is still great lack of material in the form in which we want it, from which to acquire accurate information and deduce correct principles. That side of naval history which is concerned with the conduct of the naval share in the wars of the past is still inadequately written for our purposes. Many important wars are still untouched in the more accurate method of the modern historian ; fields of research which were closed to Campbell, Lediard, and others are now available, and a new light can be thrown on these past wars by their means. The older histories are, therefore, insufficient for our purposes, and require to be supplemented by the fruits of further investigations. I wish to try to show in what points many of the available histories are deficient—and even if they were not, it must be remembered that a large proportion of them are comparatively rare books which are out of the reach of many of us.

For the sake of convenience, let me suppose that a war is to be studied. I do not wish to give the impression that this is the only use to which naval history can be put, but I take it merely as an example : what is applicable in this case is equally applicable to other fields of naval research. In the first place it is essential that all the forces—naval, military, and diplomatic—that took part should be associated. This is not to say that we require detailed description in a naval history of military operations or of politics, but we require to understand so much of them as have influenced the course of naval work. While a general history treats of naval operations only so far as their results have influenced the general situation in conjunction with all the other forces that are at play, the naval history shows also how those results were achieved.

Thus the circumstances that led up to the war should be made clear in broad outline—detail is not necessary. Rights and wrongs matter little, I apprehend, to us, who, as Blake said, have no concern with them ; but we do want to know what the war is about, for unless the aim of the combatants is known, it is clearly impossible to understand the plans made by each side to gain that end.

It is not, however, the plans alone that we wish to know. In order to understand them, the factors that led to their making should also be set out, and this in the older histories is very insufficiently done. There is rarely, if ever, a straight issue between navy and navy, or fleet and fleet. Every kind of complication affects their freedom of action. Political circumstances, external and internal, may hamper it. When I say hamper, I say it in no complaining sense— it is in the nature of things that when more than one influence has to be considered there cannot be complete freedom of action along any one line. This is too frequently overlooked. Thus the failure of the expedition to Cartagena, under Vernon and Wentworth, is a well-worn theme to illustrate the lack of co-operation between the Army and Navy. It might even better be employed as an example of the hampering effects of foreign relations. The failure was as much, if not more, due to the atittude taken up by a neutral power, France, than to any disagreement between Vernon and Wentworth on subjects ranging from the proper mode of taking a fortress to the question of whether the sailors should catch turtles for the soldiers to eat. The sailing of the expedition from England was delayed owing to the threatening attitude of France. On arrival in the West Indies, a French squadron hovering in the vicinity prevented the expedition from going direct to its objective. Put out of consideration for the moment whether it was right for the admiral to go to Port Louis to attack the French, and remember only that the fact of the French being there made him go—that they exercised this influence on his movements. These delays made the operations late in beginning; the rainy season came on before the place was taken; the men were dying by hundreds because of the hindrances put on the starting of the expedition—and its subsequent failure was partly, though not altogether, due to the attitude of a foreign power. A modern instance of a singularly similar nature occurred before the Russo-Japanese war; the Russian plans (so the Russian official history tells us) were affected by the fear of what a squadron of a certain neutral power might do.

Internal politics no less have their effect. At the time of that same expedition of Vernon's there was disaffection in this country. The ministry were afraid of the Jacobites—a Jacobite rising was the perpetual bugbear. One result of this was that the troops sent consisted very largely of men newly raised in England or North America—a fact which unquestionably affected the operations. Similarly, the attempted invasions of 1744 or 1745 would by themselves have been by no means so dangerous if the Jacobite unrest had not been connected with the campaigns. A smaller force was required to upset the kingdom, and the difficulty of dealing with the attempt was by that increased. Numbers which in ordinary circumstances could have achieved little, became of importance when they might be joined by disaffected persons in England. The naval operations in the narrow seas were proportionately affected by this.

The practical value of these examples is, that we can apply their lessons to our conditions of to-day, and ask ourselves—is there anything analogous in the political or social conditions of to-day, which might prejudice the freedom of employment of our forces, within or without the kingdom ?

These points are brought out in few of the older histories that I have read, yet they are essential to a correct understanding of every war, and therefore a history which does not refer to them is incomplete and misleading.

The next point on which our histories give us insufficient information is the orders and instructions on which our admirals were working—not only indeed insufficient, but frequently inaccurate information. Turning again to Vernon, it is a repeated fable that he was sent out to capture Portobello—yet the word Portobello neither in fact nor by inference ever occurs in his instructions, and until he reached Jamaica his intention was to proceed to Havana and blockade the galleons.

I think it worth while to point out these things ; for if one does not know the instructions on which an admiral is acting, how can one judge whether he is carrying them out well or ill ? The historian of the past lived perhaps too near the events to be able to get the true instructions —they could not then be made public. Occasionally, too often indeed, the true instructions leaked out through the mouths of garrulous ministers ; but sometimes they did not, and our historical ancestors seem then to have contented themselves with inventing what appeared to be likely instructions.

In one old book I have even found the chronicler gravely laying it down that fleets frequently went to sea in war with no instructions at all, but sailed, as you might say, for the sake of sailing. What is the distracted would-be student to do when he reads that kind of thing? He naturally draws the conclusion that naval history is of no practical value, for it is clear to him that such an explanation is outside the realms of possibility and cannot be true.

When we know the instructions, we next want to see how the admiral proceeded to carry them out. What were the claims upon him? Besides the enemy's fleet, what other influences had he to reckon with? Movements of armies, protection of trade, trouble with neutrals, half-hearted allies, insufficient supplies, shortage of men, interfering ministers—all these influenced his movements. Played on a chess-board, the game may be simple enough; played with these distractions it is a different matter; and if they are not alluded to and brought out, the whole thing will be in false perspective.

These and others were the influences that so often forced us to fight at a disadvantage, and not, as some would have it, a natural preference for engaging with inferior numbers.

False ideas have thus obtained credence because the historian has not thrown his investigating net wide enough. What we want is a picture of the conflicting elements which an admiral had before him; let us see him in the middle of his distractions; point out to us the information, or the lack of information, on which he had to act. So far as is possible, put us in his position and make us think what we ourselves should have done. This will give us a true idea of war —war as it really is, with the drawn curtain hiding the enemy's movements. Criticism of what a commander did should, if it is to be of any value to a student, be based on the information that commander had at the time, and not on information placed subsequently at our disposal.

Mr Fortescue's description of the Corunna campaign is one which I have ventured to admire greatly : the picture it gives of Napoleon receiving the news of Moore's advance, the Emperor's uncertainty as to what it meant, at what it was aimed, give one the liveliest idea of the kind of situation in which a commander, whether at sea or on land, may find himself.

Next as to the operations themselves. There are instances of histories—James is an example, but there are others—in which we find operations divided into two categories, " major " and " minor." Fleet actions generally are classed as major—all others as minor. This is supremely misleading ; for the man who wishes to understand war it makes history hopeless. Let me again give an example.

It is a well-known thing that practically the biggest task the Navy has had to perform in the wars of the past has been the protection of trade.

Yet how much do we find references to this in the older histories ? We find isolated squadron actions in the Soundings referred to ; the details of the action described—the wind, the sea, the sail carried, the weight of the broadsides, the number of guns on each side—and perhaps some scathingly contemptuous criticism of the commander is indulged in. But we are not told why the squadron was there, what function it was performing ; and, although often enough it was one element in the wide flung system of trade protection, it is relegated to the category of a minor operation.

The protection of trade, it is hardly necessary to remark, is a major operation of the highest importance, and it is essential to co-ordinate these cruiser operations in order to understand it. Yet, except for stray references to convoys, to losses by privateers, and to captures of enemy's trade in cruising vessels, our stock histories tell us next to nothing. The system—the essential thing—is not brought out.

I have still another instance in my mind of the same heresy of classifying operations in which the proceedings of a fleet of over sixty ships in the Mediterranean, of which forty were ships of force, are treated under the heading of " minor operations."

This fleet was in these waters at a time when England was believed to be seriously threatened with invasion—is it comprehensible that such a large force would be abroad, engaged in a minor operation, at a period when the national security was endangered ? Of course not ; and when we examine the actual function of that fleet we find that it was acting in conjunction with great armies, and assisting to preserve the north of Italy from invasion. If that fleet had left the Mediterranean the effect of its departure would have been felt from Naples to Flanders. The classification of such an operation as a minor one distorts the view and gives a wholly wrong impression of the employment of the naval forces at that time.

In most of the older naval histories the battle plays the great part. Everything is centred round the battle, and indeed, inasmuch as the battle is the final settlement of a situation, this is but natural. But do not let the historian lose sight of the relation between the battle and the other operations ; it is not the battle that brings the enemy to a peace ; it is the action which that battle permits the winner to take and which the loser is unable to prevent. The battle is like a severe surgical operation—it is carried out to relieve a situation which has become too painful to be borne ; or it may be carried out to prevent such a situation from arising. It is the employment of the naval forces generally that is worrying the enemy. He cannot carry on his

D

trade, he cannot send his troops by sea—the highway of the waters is in hostile hands, and he cannot use it ; he seeks to relieve the pressure by a battle.

Although, therefore, the battle is the final arbitrament and the means of solution, it is the operations of blockade, commerce attack and military invasion that are distressing him. We must not lose sight of this in writing and studying history. Following my previous method, I would point out an example of the kind of error that arises from this lack of proportion.

The British fleet in the Mediterranean referred to before was conducting a blockade of the coasts of Catalonia, Provence, Genoa, and Naples. It prevented French and Spanish troops from passing by sea into Italy. The inland routes, the difficult alpine passes, were held by armies, the roads by the coast were under the guns of the small ships of the British fleet. The situation was, from the Franco-Spanish point of view, intolerable, and, to relieve it, an allied fleet, nearly equal in strength, put to sea to drive the British fleet from the coast. The fleets fought. The Allies retreated to the coast of Spain, having lost one ship; three more had fled from the action, and the two squadrons of which the fleet was composed parted company. The British fleet after a short absence, of which the enemy temporarily availed himself, returned to the Riviera and resumed its blockade.

I have seen descriptions of this action in which it was said that it was indecisive for the British, and that the fruits of victory were left in the hands of the enemy. Other descriptions allude to the battle as equivalent to a British defeat. Indecisive the action certainly was, but I suggest that the other descriptions are not fit to apply to an action, of which, however little the British fleet may have succeeded in destroying the enemy, the results were that the enemy failed entirely to do what it came out to do —remove the blockade and pass its troops into Italy by the sea route. In consequence of this action, the attack on Lombardy had to be undertaken by land : the influence on the campaign was inestimable.

In describing the battle, let us know, as in the strategy, whether the admiral had a clear field in which to work. Were there any strategic or other considerations which influenced his conduct in the preliminaries of the battle, the battle itself, the retreat or the pursuit ? I can call to mind two actions—the battle referred to above, and another in the Russo-Japanese war, in which other considerations besides crushing the enemy were in the admiral's mind. It may be the admirals were right or wrong in allowing themselves to be affected by these influences ; but in

judging of the matter we must know, as much as
we can, what those influences were, if history
is going to be of any practical value to us. We
have Admiral Mahan's authority that it can be
so. Historical instances, he says, are by their
concrete force worth a ream of dissertation.
Let us, therefore, have the instances set out as
freely as possible to show us with what difficulties
the admiral had to contend, what were his per-
plexities in regard to engaging or not engaging,
pursuing or forbearing to pursue, and so on, and
how he decided to solve them. They may serve
us as a precedent if we should find ourselves at
some time in a like case.

While history will help us in situations of a
strategic nature, so also it provides mental food
of a tactical kind. The description of a battle
which brings out the situations that arose whilst
it was in progress, and how these situations were
met, affords us invaluable lessons ; for though the
difference between sail and steam affects such
details as speed, range, and other factors, the
main issues will often be comparable. Napoleon
is said to have remarked that the happiest
inspiration upon the battlefield was often only a
recollection ; but besides providing us perhaps
with one of the happy inspirations, the way in
which a situation was met generally brings out
something of the trend of thought of the day,
and the theory of command, that supremely

important matter as held in that particular fleet.

I say advisedly fleet, for the same theories did not necessarily pervade the whole service. A doctrine of unquestioning adhesion to a rigid formula, by which no one is allowed to move without orders from a central source, may be held in one fleet, while in another at the same period individuality of action may be encouraged.

It will be true that one doctrine or the other has the greater hold in the service, but history will be false to itself if it does not bring out something both of the trend of naval thought, and of the personalities of the commanders ; showing us those who translated instructions literally, and those who could translate them in the spirit, and the effect on the conduct of the operations of the mental attitude of each class of commander.

Besides giving us an accurate presentment of facts, I hope historians will not shrink from drawing conclusions from those facts. I think their work would be robbed of a great deal of its value if they were to refrain from doing so. In the course of their investigations they will of necessity have examined a great mass of material, which, though it serves to build up their conclusions, cannot be included in their text. If in their books they will give us so much of this as will serve to justify their conclusions, we, the students, will be furnished not only with some material from which to draw our own, but will also have our attention drawn to points which, by their prominence in the original manuscripts, have convinced the writers that they influenced the operations in a certain manner ; they will thus serve as a starting point for more discussion and so further one of the important aims of historical study, which is to make one think.

Finally, let me remind the historian that it is to him we look to give us the means of informing ourselves. As in economic life the raw material of one man is the finished article of another, so it is in history. The historian's raw material lies out of reach of the naval officer in the museums, the public and the private collections. His finished article is the history ; and this history is the raw material on which *we* have to build up our finished article, which is our knowledge of war. Let the historian provide us with this raw material, so complete, so accurate, and so presented, that the naval officer may be sure he is building up his knowledge upon a sound foundation.

SAMUEL PEPYS AS A NAVAL OFFICIAL

BY DR J. R. TANNER

HISTORY has long done full justice to the Samuel
Pepys who reveals himself in the *Diary*, but
historians have sometimes underestimated the
importance of the long official career of which
the *Diary* was only a bye-product. This career
was efficient, and even distinguished, in a high
degree; and its merits can only be properly
appreciated if allowance is made for the difficulties which had to be encountered by the
naval administrator of Pepys's day.

Some of these difficulties were of the nature
of an inheritance, for the disease of the Restoration period had already declared itself before
the Restoration took place. The earlier govern-
ments of the Interregnum were well financed,
but to a certain extent they were living upon
capital—the capital represented by confiscations
and Royalist compositions. Thus towards the
end of the period the pressure of financial difficulties began to be felt, and three months before
the king came back the debts of the Navy stood at
a million and a quarter.[1] The Navy " is in very sad

[1] *Calendar of State Papers, Domestic*, 1659-60, p. 383.

condition," wrote Pepys in the *Diary*, as early as 31st July 1660, "and money must be raised for it."

The financial problem with which Pepys and his colleagues were faced was difficult in time of peace, but when the Second Dutch War broke out, in the spring of 1665, the situation, in spite of large Parliamentary grants, soon became very serious. The cost of the Navy in peace time was about £400,000 a year.[1] A paper in the Pepysian Library [2] estimates the cost of the twenty-five months from 1st Sept. 1664 to 29th Sept. 1666 at £3,200,516, of which £930,496 remained as a debt; and this debt had risen by the end of the war to £1,100,000.[3] Similar details are not available for the Third Dutch War, although there are many references to shortness of money, and it is known that the want of men and of materials for speedy refitting occasioned the loss of nearly six weeks in the best season of the year, and so interfered with the success of the naval operations of 1673.[4] Later on the financial situation improved greatly, and a statement of the Navy debt remaining unpaid in January 1687 entered in the Pepysian *Miscellanies*,[5] shews only £171,836, 2s. 9d. still outstanding.

The consequences of financial pressure worked

---

[1] *Catalogue of Pepysian MSS.*, i. 100 (*Navy Records Society*, vol. xxvi.).

[2] *Pepysian MSS.*, No. 2589, p. 13.

[3] *Cal. S. P., Dom.*, 1667, p. 471.

[4] *Cal. S. P. Dom.*, 1673, p. x.   [5] xi. 18.

themselves out in many disastrous ways. One commissioner wrote that the country was " shy,"[1] and another that all men distrust "London pay."[2] The result was that bargains were lost for want of ready money,[3] and where credit was obtained, enormous prices had to be paid. Nearly half the letters to the Navy Commissioners in the State Papers calendared for 1665-6 refer to the difficulties experienced by government agents in obtaining supplies.[4] Another wasteful consequence of the want of money is referred to by Pepys at the end of the Third Dutch War. In a letter to the Navy Board he writes of " that mighty charge which has so long lain upon our hands for want of money to discharge those of the ships which remain yet unpaid off."[5] There were, however, two important departments of naval administration which were completely wrecked for want of money—victualling and pay.

In 1665 the victualling system broke down completely — partly owing to the contractor's delays in delivery, and partly in consequence of the badness of the provisions themselves. Some of the complaints of quality are not without a humorous aspect. On 10th August Commissioner Middleton writes to Pepys from Portsmouth that

[1] S. P. Dom., Car. II., cii. 123.
[2] Cal. S. P. Dom., 1665-6, p. 189.
[3] Ibid., 1666-7, p. 228 ; 1665-6, p. 189.
[4] Ibid., 1665-6, p. xxxix.
[5] Admiralty Letters, viii. 403 (8th Dec. 1678).

the " Coventry " was still in port ; her beer had
nearly poisoned one man who, "being thirsty,
drank a great draught."[1] Even after the new
victualling contract of 1677 we hear constant
complaints of the victuals supplied under it.
" The serving of the king's ships with shanks,"
writes Pepys,[2] has " always been excepted
against, and yet if my information be true, no
less than 21 legs was found in 58 pieces of beef
lately delivered on board the ' Cambridge,' and
bread so mouldy as that within 5 or 6 days'
time the poor men were forced to cut away
above $\frac{1}{3}$ of it before it was fit to be eaten, by
reason of its mouldiness." A little later there are
complaints of the " ill quality of the brandy."[3]

Complaints of quality must not be taken
quite at their face value, for we have the same
sort of thing in the best days of Commonwealth administration.[4] In 1653 the officers
of the "Seven Brothers" certified that the fish
on board stank and was unfit to eat, while
the beef also was in a doubtful state.[5] In
another case the beer was so bad that it
had to be thrown overboard.[6] A month later

[1] S. P. Dom., Car. II., cxxviii. 85. Cf. Cal. S. P., Dom., 1664-5,
p. 480.
[2] Admiralty Letters, vii. 153.
[3] Ibid., vii. 391.
[4] Cal. S. P. Dom., 1652-3, p. 35 ; vols. 1653-4 and 1654 passim.
See also Oppenheim, The Administration of the Royal Navy, p. 326.
[5] Cal. S. P. Dom., 1652-3, p. 577.
[6] Ibid., p. 590.

the generals at sea complained of "stinking
beer," of "salt beer which causes sickness,"
and of "mouldy bread from Hull."[1] In the
same year Captain John Taylor, the master
shipwright at Chatham, attributed the delay in
the despatch of the ships from thence to the
victuals—"beer, bread, and butter worse than I
ever saw in the dearest times."[2] A captain
brought his ship into Spithead because "the
beer stinks, which has caused many men to fall
sick and others to run, and the butter and other
provisions are as bad as they can be."[3] It may
not have been this which accounted for "strange
fits, like convulsions or calenture," which seized
twenty of a ship's company in 1654,[4] but John
Hollond doubted "whether the sword of the
Dutch or the want and badness of provisions did
most execution upon our men in the late wars,"[5]
and the Navy Commissioners themselves admitted
in their official correspondence that "unwhole-
some provisions hazard men's lives."[6]

But defects in quality were perhaps less important than delays in delivery, which seriously
interfered with the readiness and efficiency of
the fighting fleets. In 1668 men were deserting

---

[1] *Cal. S. P. Dom.*, 1652-3, p. 428.
[2] *Ibid.*, 1653-4, p. 20.
[3] *Ibid.*, p. 465 ; see also pp. 478, 480, 582.
[4] *Ibid.*, 1654, p. 580.
[5] *Discourses*, p. 157.
[6] *Cal. S. P., Dom.*, 1654, p. 380.

from the ships because they could get no food.[1]
In 1673, during the Third Dutch War, Prince
Rupert was so annoyed at the want of provisions
when the fleet returned to the Nore in June,
that he declared he would never thrive at sea
till some were hanged on land ;[2] and a little
later he wrote to Lord Arlington that there was
no way with the victuallers but to send Mr Child
or Mr Papillon on shipboard, there to stay in
what condition his Majesty shall think fitting,
till they have thoroughly victualled the fleet.[3]
In 1678 Pepys, in a letter to the Navy Officers,
refers to the " backwardness " of the victuallers
as " that great point which gives both you and
me so much pain," [4] and again later as " matter
of mighty affliction " [5] to himself.　In 1679 Sir
Robert Robinson's fleet for the West was delayed
" many days " at Portsmouth, which led Pepys
to declare, " I know not how possibly to lament
enough the wretched state his Majesty's service
must be in while it lies under this uncertainty of
being supplied with stores and provisions " at this
port, and to admit at the same time " the yet
greater uncertainty of . . . meeting with any
despatch at Plymouth." [6]

[1] *Cal. S. P. Dom.*, 1667-8, p. xviii.
[2] *Ibid.*, 1673, p. xi.
[3] *Ibid.*, p. 384.
[4] *Admiralty Letters*, viii. 365.
[5] *Ibid.*, viii. 370.
[6] *Ibid.*, ix. 140, 142.

And yet the punctual supply of good victuals to the Navy was a vital matter. Pepys the official comments on this with the same shrewdness which characterised Pepys of the *Diary*. "Englishmen," he says in his *Naval Minutes*, "and more especially seamen, love their Bellies above anything else, and therefore it must always be remembered in the management of the victualling of the Navy, that to make any abatement from them in the quantity or agreeableness of the victuals is to discourage and provoke them in the tenderest point, and will sooner render them disgusted with the king's service than any one other hardship that can be put upon them." [1]

Pepys made desperate efforts to secure better supervision over quality, but the problem was not really an administrative one. It is clear from the references in the *Admiralty Letters* and elsewhere that the source of the evil lay in a region where the administrator was powerless—in the region of finance. The case is stated by the contractors themselves in a letter to the Navy Board dated 5th April 1671,[2] and to this argument there could be no answer. "We have not only exceedingly suffered in losing the opportunities of providing and saving of victuals in the most seasonable and cheapest times of the year . . . but his

---

[1] *Pepysian MSS.*, No. 2866, p. 274.
[2] *S. P. Dom.*, Car. II., ccxcix. 105.

Majesty's service is daily under manifold incon-
veniencies for want of victuals to be always in a
readiness both for the sea and harbour, which we
are no ways able to prevent without we have
payment as the contract doth direct. . . . Without those supplies of money as are needful and
the contract provides for . . . we are not able
to supply his Majesty's ships any longer with
victuals, either in harbour or at sea, nor discharge
those foreign bills that have been drawn on and
accepted by us for his Majesty's service, the want
of punctual payment of which . . . is a manifold
mischief to his Majesty's service."

A similar condition of things prevailed in
the matter of pay. An entry in the *Diary* on
this subject brings out incidentally one of the
diarist's most attractive qualities—his genuine
feeling for the poor seaman. Under date 7th
Oct. 1665 he writes : " Did business, though not
much, at the office; because of the horrible crowd
and lamentable moan of the poor seamen that
lie starving in the streets for lack of money.
Which do trouble and perplex me to the heart ;
and more at noon when we were to go through
them, for then a whole hundred of them followed
us ; some cursing, some swearing, and some pray-
ing to us." A month later, on 4th Nov., he is
less sympathetic. " After dinner I to the office
and there late, and much troubled to have 100
seamen all the afternoon there, swearing below

and cursing us, and breaking the glass windows, and swear they will pull the house down on Tuesday next. I sent word of this to Court, but nothing will help it but money and a rope."

We hear of wages 22,[1] 34[2] and even 52[3] months in arrear. One captain complains that for want of pay "instead of a young commander" he "is rendered an old beggar."[4] The crews of two ships petition the Navy Board to order them their pay "that their families may not be altogether starved in the streets, and themselves go like heathens, having nothing to cover their nakedness."[3] The commissioner at Portsmouth writes of workmen in the yard there—"Turned out of doors by their landlords, they perish more like dogs than men."[5] Naturally enough, this state of things affected discipline. The Chatham shipwrights and caulkers, to whom two years' wages were owing, marched up to London to appeal to the Navy Board, as "their families are denied trust and cannot subsist," and under this pressure arrangements were made, with a reckless disregard of their moral effect, "to pay off some of the most disorderly."[6] At Woolwich

[1] Cal. S. P. Dom., 1667, p. 46.
[2] Ibid., p. 75.
[3] Ibid., p. lx note.
[4] Ibid., 1665-6, p. 385.
[5] Ibid., 1664-5, p. 522.
[6] Ibid., 1667-8, p. xiv.

the men struck work ;[1] and from Chatham the
commissioner writes : " I am almost torn to pieces
by the workmen of the yard for their weekly
pay."[2]   At Portsmouth the officer in charge
writes for money to be sent immediately to stop
the " bawlings and impatience " of the men,
and especially of their wives, " whose tongues,"
he says, " are as foul as the daughters of Billings-
gate."[3]   Later on there was a mutiny there,
but Commissioner Middleton shewed a praise-
worthy promptitude in dealing with it. He
" seized a good cudgel out of the hands of one of
the men, and took more pains in the use of it
than in any business for the last 12 months."
He adds that he " has not been troubled since."[4]
Even the peace with Holland did not put an
end to these disorders, for the financial position
of the Navy was not greatly improved.   In March
1671 the shipwrights and caulkers of Deptford
" fell " on Mr Bagwell, the foreman of the yard,
"and it was God's great mercy they had not
spoiled him."[5]

If historians sometimes underestimate Pepys's
difficulties, readers of the *Diary* have a way of
underestimating Pepys.   They are under a standing
misapprehension about his age, and speak of him

[1] *Cal. S. P. Dom.*, 1667-8, p. xiv.
[2] *Ibid.*, 1667-8, p. 443.
[3] *Ibid.*, 1664-5, p. 475.
[4] *Ibid.*, 1665-6, p. 53.
[5] *S. P. Dom.*, Car. II., ccxcvii. 19.

as " poor old Pepys " or " good old Pepys "—
the amusing elderly gentleman whose chief claim
on posterity lies in the fact that he gave himself
away more completely and more engagingly than
anyone else has ever done before or since. But this
is to forget that Pepys was not twenty-seven when
he began the *Diary*, and only thirty-six when he
gave up writing on account of his eyesight, saying
that to do so is "almost as much as to see myself go
into my grave." But he lived to be seventy years
of age, and although he was only a public servant
for part of that time, he certainly became during
his two secretaryships, what Monck had called
him earlier, perhaps only in compliment, " the
right hand of the Navy." [1] The maturity of his
powers lies outside the period of the *Diary*, and
it is his later life that makes good his claim to
be regarded as one of the best public officials who
ever served the State.

There is abundant material in the Pepysian
Library at Cambridge for supplementing the
impression of Pepys's character and powers which
the *Diary* affords us, and in particular the 15,000
letters which constitute his official correspondence during his tenure of the office of Secretary
of the Admiralty, from 1673 to 1679 and again
from 1684 to 1688. His vitality of character
and variety of interests appear in the *Diary*,
but from these sources we get something different ;

[1] *Diary*, 24th April 1665.

E

for in a document which is so true to human nature as the *Diary*, it is almost inevitable that the diarist, although sufficiently self-satisfied, should be quite unconscious of his strongest points. We should expect business habits from a government official, but in his correspondence Pepys exhibits a methodical devotion to business which is beyond praise. We have here sobriety and soundness of judgment ; a sense of the paramount importance of discipline, and the exercise of a steady pressure upon others to restore it in the Navy ; a high standard of personal duty, which permits no slackness and spares no pains ; and a remarkable capacity for tactful diplomacy. The decorous self-satisfaction of the *Diary* has been replaced in later years by professional pride ; and an outlook upon business affairs which had always been intelligent has become profoundly serious. The agreeable vices of the *Diary* suggest the light, irresponsible cavalier. The correspondence suggests that Pepys was a Puritan at heart, although without the Puritan rigidity of practice or narrowness of view. In his professional career he exhibits precisely those virtues which had made the naval administration of the earlier Commonwealth a success—the virtues of the Independent colonels who manned the offices during the First Dutch War. The change is that from the rather dissolute-looking young Royalist painted by

Lely to the ample wig and pursed official lips of the Kneller portrait ; although the subject's advance in visible virtue is quite consistent with a sad backsliding in the art which depicts him.

That Pepys was a disciplinarian appears everywhere in the official correspondence. He had a high sense of the honour of the service, and showed himself at once firm and humane in his dealings with those who were under his authority. He was at great pains to keep himself well informed of the proceedings of the captains, urging the Navy Board, where it appeared to them that captains were "not so steady in their attendance on and solicitous for the despatch of their ships fitting forth as their duty obligeth them" to "be at the trouble of advertising" him.[1] Where breaches of discipline were reported to him he took the greatest pains to arrive at the facts, and when they occurred in foreign ports this often involved him in an immense amount of correspondence.

One frequent cause of complaint was the practice by which captains, in defiance of the regulations, appeared "daily in the town" without leave ; and on July 9th, 1675, Pepys himself "spied" the captain of the Lark "at a distance sauntering up and down Covent Garden."[2] Three years later the trouble was worse, and Pepys remarks,[3]

---

[1] *Admiralty Letters*, iv. 191. [2] *Ibid.*, iv. 178.
[3] *Ibid.*, vi. 480.

" I must confess I have never observed so frequent and scandalous instances as I do this day by commanders hovering daily about the Court and town, though without the least pretence for it." " Pray think of it and help me herein," he writes a little later to Sir Thomas Allin,[1] " for, as I shall never be guilty of withstanding any gentleman's just occasions and desires in this matter, so I shall never be able to sit still and silent under the scandalous liberties that I see every day taken by commanders of playing with his Majesty's service, as if it were an indifferent matter whether they give any attendance on board their ships, so as they have their wages as if they did." The result of his deliberations was that in April 1679, the Lords of the Admiralty resolved "most fervently to rectify this evil with all the strictness that may be,"[2] and on the advice of Pepys they decided that leave should only be granted to captains in the future under the hand either of the king or of themselves—" I having shown them," he writes, " that whatever is less than that is too little."[3] Unfortunately for this decision, a disastrous change of administration was at hand, and Pepys was soon to be driven from office by the Popish Plot.

After Pepys's return to office in 1684, we find him engaged in a crusade against drunkenness,

---

[1] *Admiralty Letters*, vii. 296.　　　[2] *Ibid.*, ix. 220.
[3] *Ibid.*, ix. 220.

laying down sound principles in admirably chosen terms. In one case, where an old offender's captain had suggested that removal to another ship would be sufficient punishment, Pepys pressed for dismissal, since " he whose debauchery renders him unfit for any one charge in the Navy, renders himself by the same means unfit for every other, and therefore, unfit for one unfit for all, there being no office so little in the Navy but requires and deserves sobriety to manage it as it ought to be managed for the king." [1] " Till that vice be cured," he writes a few months later (4th Feb. 1685),[2] . . . " I do despair of ever seeing his Majesty's service therein to thrive, and as I have given one or two instances of my care therein already, so shall I not fail by the grace of God to persevere in it as far as I am able, till it be thoroughly cured, let it light where it will."

An illustration of Pepys's diplomatic skill may be found in the method he adopted to induce James II. in 1686 to appoint to his new commission for naval reform the great shipbuilder, Sir Anthony Deane. He furnished the king with a list of the principal shipbuilders of England, and after respectfully dismissing Sir John Tippetts and Sir Phineas Pett as disqualified by age and infirmity,[3] he deals with the rest in

[1] *Admiralty Letters*, x. 137.   [2] *Ibid.*, x. 310.
[3] *Catalogue of Pepysian MSS.*, i. 77.

such a manner as to lead irresistibly to the desired conclusion that Deane was indispensable. We are admitted to a gallery of pen-and-ink sketches touched off by a master-hand.[1]

Mr Lee, the master-shipwright at Chatham, " never built a ship in his life . . . he is also full of the gout, and by consequence " not capable of fatigue. Mr Betts at Portsmouth has built several good ships, but is " illiterate, and not of countenance, method, or authority sufficient for a commissioner of the Navy, especially in this post." Mr John Shish at Deptford is " old Jonas Shish's son, as illiterate as he . . . low-spirited, of little appearance or authority . . . little frugality ; " his father " a great drinker, and since killed with it." Mr Lawrence at Woolwich " has never built a ship in his life but the ' Little Victory,' which he rebuilt at great charge, and when done was found fit for nothing but a fire-ship. A low-spirited, slow, and gouty man . . . illiterate and supine to the last degree." Mr Furzer at Sheerness is " young " and " never built a ship . . . always bred under his father ; working little, and thereby as little acquainted in the methods of good husbandry." Mr Dummer, assistant shipwright at Chatham, is " an ingenious young man, but said rarely to have handled a tool in his life ; " a mere draughtsman. Mr Pett, another assistant at Chatham, and son of Sir

[1] *Pepysian MSS.*, No. 1490, p. 145.

Phineas Pett, is " one that loves his ease, as having been ever used to it, not knowing what it is to work or take pains . . . bred always in the king's service within doors, and very debauched." Mr Stiggant, assistant at Portsmouth, is only a boatbuilder. Mr Harding, assistant at Deptford, is " a very slow man, of no learning, authority, or countenance, nor ever built a ship in his life." Passing outside the king's service, Sir H. Johnson at Blackwall is " an ingenious young gentleman, but above all personal labour, as being left too well provided for to work much." Mr Collins, his partner, is " a good and painful, but very plain and illiterate man; a Phanatick; of no authority or countenance." Mr Robert Castle at Deptford " has built many and very good merchant ships." He is " a good fellow, gouty, and too much engaged in merchant business to be able presently to withdraw from it, were he otherwise qualified for this occasion." Of the four Thames shipwrights remaining on the list, Mr Graves, though a good builder, is " illiterate, of little presence, very old ; " the other, Jonas Shish, like his brother, is " illiterate, low-spirited, and of no countenance," and labours under the additional disqualification of having never built anything but merchantmen ; Mr Barham is " above threescore years old . . . a man of no spirit nor method, and a Phanatick ; " and Mr Narbrough, though " a person of the best appearance of all the merchant builders, and a man of good sense," has "but little experience, and that chiefly in small craft."

This appalling list of disqualifications had the effect it was designed to have upon the king's mind ; it induced "full conviction of the necessity of his prevailing with and satisfying Sir A. D."[1] The precise terms that were offered him do not transpire, but on Saturday, 13th March, Mr Pepys brought Sir Anthony Deane "to the king in the morning to kiss his hand, who declared the same to him to his full satisfaction, and afterwards to my lord treasurer at the treasury chamber, with the same mutual content."[2]

The papers in the Pepysian Library teem with illustrations of the business instincts and orderly habits of Pepys as a naval administrator. During his tenure of office the practice of the Navy in various departments was reduced to a methodical "establishment." In 1673 an "establishment of cabins" was adopted,[3] which has proved of special interest to naval archæologists for the light it throws on the internal arrangements and accommodation of warships during the period. In 1677 Pepys himself drew up an establishment "for ascertaining the duty of a sea-lieutenant, and for examining persons pretending to that office,"[4] and this was adopted

---

[1] *Pepysian MSS.*, No. 1490, p. 16.   [2] *Ibid.*, p. 17.
[3] *Pepysian MSS.*, No. 2867, *Naval Precedents*, p. 478.
[4] *Pepysian MSS.*, No. 2867, *Naval Precedents*, p. 241.

by the authorities without substantial alteration.[1] Candidates were required to be of twenty years of age at the least and to have served three years actually at sea. Provision was also made for a "solemn examination," to be held at the Navy Office, of the aspirant's "ability to judge of and perform the duty of an able seaman and midshipman, and his having attained to a sufficient degree of knowledge in the theory of navigation capacitating him thereto." In this examination candidates were sometimes ploughed; and Pepys describes the system later as an encouragement to the "true-bred seaman," and greatly to the benefit of the king's service; "for I thank God," he writes,[2] "we have not half the throng of those of the bastard breed pressing for employments which we heretofore used to be troubled with, they being conscious of their inability to pass this examination, and know it to be to no purpose now to solicit for employment till they have done it." A reform of this kind, when its consequences had time to work themselves out, must have gone far to end the standing controversy between "gentlemen" and "tarpaulin" commanders.

Another establishment of 1677 placed on a better footing the provision of chaplains for the service of the Navy [3]—none being appointed in future but such as could produce a written

[1] *Admiralty Letters*, vi. 256.   [2] *Ibid.*, vii. 17.
[3] *Pepysian MSS.*, No. 2867, *Naval Precedents*, p. 161.

certificate, under the hand of either the Arch-
bishop of Canterbury or the Bishop of London,
testifying to the " piety, learning, conformity,
and other the qualifications of the said person
fitting him for the said charge." This also
originated with Pepys himself, who designed it to
remedy " the ill-effects of the looseness wherein
that matter lay, with respect both to the honour
of God Almighty and the preservation of sobriety
and good discipline in his Majesty's fleet."[1]

The important year 1677 also saw the adoption
of " An establishment of men and guns to the
whole Royal Navy of England,"[2] intended for " a
solemn, universal, and unalterable adjustment of
the gunning and manning of the whole fleet (otherwise than by order of the King and Council) ; "[3]
and the chief credit of it was claimed by Pepys.

In the short reign of James II. the framing and
revising of " establishments " was carried further
still. An important new departure is to be
found in the " establishment about plate carriage
and allowance for captains' tables "[4] dated 15th
July 1686, which was an attempt to revive
discipline in the Navy by giving the Admiralty a
ready control over ships on foreign service, and
at the same time so to improve the financial
position of the captains as to put them beyond

[1] *Admiralty Letters*, vi. 18, 45.
[2] *Pepysian MSS.*, No. 1340.]
[3] *Pepysian MSS.*, No. 2867, *Naval Precedents*, p. 210.
[4] *Ibid.*, p. 245.

the reach of temptations to neglect public duty for private gain. A feature of this is the requirement that admirals' orders for the proceeding of ships on any service must be in writing, a copy being sent to the Secretary of the Admiralty both by the superior giving the order and the inferior receiving it ; that commanders touching at foreign ports are to send from each to the Secretary of the Admiralty "abstracts of their journals" and " a particular account of their proceedings ; " and that they shall deliver to the Secretary at the end of each voyage " an entire book containing a perfect journal thereof, together with a book of entries to be kept of all orders either issued or received." The delivery of journals was not in itself a novelty, but the existing practice of the Navy was systematised and improved upon in Pepys's methodical way.

In the year 1686 also we come upon an elaborate establishment concerning " volunteers and midshipmen extraordinary,"[1] based upon an earlier scheme of 1676 designed to afford encouragement " to families of better quality . . . to breed up their younger sons to the art and practice of navigation " by " the bearing several young gentlemen to the ends aforesaid " on board the king's ships as " volunteers," and to provide employment for ex-commanders or lieutenants, by carrying them as " midshipmen extraordinary "

---

[1] *Pepysian MSS.*, No. 2867, *Naval Precedents*, p. 156.

over and above the complement established for the ships in which they sailed.

Another establishment of this period is that for boatswains' and carpenters' sea-stores,[1] drafted by the Navy Board in November 1686. It had come under the notice of the Board that no uniform establishment of this kind had ever before been made, " but that the same have been for the most part issued, and their expenses allowed, at the pleasure and discretion of inferior officers in the Yards." This want of certainty had led to " unlimited and extravagant expenses " of these stores, and the Board had therefore undertaken " a deliberate consideration and adjustment of the qualities, quantities, and proportions of each distinct species of stores needful to be supplied to each ship . . . whether for an eight or twelve months voyage." For this establishment Pepys was not directly responsible, but it serves as another illustration of the care with which business principles were being applied in his time and under his influence to the organisation and administration of the Navy.

The official style of the Pepysian papers exhibits all the special characteristics of the time, carried to a high degree of excellence. We find here labyrinthine sentences, in which the thread of thought winds deviously through an infinity of dependent clauses, but always

[1] *Pepysian MSS.*, No. 2867, *Naval Precedents*, p. 639.

brings the reader in the end to the destined goal—
the deliberate selection of words that sound and
re-echo, without any sacrifice of precision of
meaning—the reader's invariable sense of something dignified moving before him, like a proces-
sion. But Pepys contributes something more than
his contemporaries, for his official correspondence
is often redeemed from dulness or ponderousness
by a sense of humour usually full-flavoured, but
on occasion as subtle and delicate as need be.
Of this a single illustration will suffice.

Sir Robert Robinson's chaplain preached a
sermon with which Sir Robert Robinson was
greatly pleased, and accordingly he sent it up to
Pepys for presentation to the Bishop of London,
who had control over the preferment of naval
chaplains.   Pepys, foreseeing, perhaps, the tide of
sermons that would begin to flow towards Fulham
if this one were accepted, did his best for the
Bishop, and that as courteously as might be.

" As for your chaplain's sermon," he writes,[1]
" were it fit for me to give him advice, it would
be that he would not have it exposed to my lord
Bishop's perusal and censure till it were fairer
writ, and writ more correctly, this being done
so slightly as to its manner of writing, and with
so many blots, interlineations, false spellings, and
wrong pointings, that I doubt, besides the prejudice
the author may receive to his credit, the Bishop

[1] *Admiralty Letters*, viii. 432.

may think himself a little neglected in his having it presented to him in no better dress, and with so many errata's. Upon which consideration I shall, in friendship to him and out of respect to you, respite the offering of it to my lord Bishop, until upon conferring with your chaplain I hear again from you about it, I being mightily of opinion that he should either have it sent him back from me to Portsmouth, there to have it well corrected by himself and got more fairly and legibly wrote, or committed to some friend of his own order and acquaintance in town who may have leisure to see it done for him. Nor do I think the gentleman will receive any considerable delay by this means to the satisfaction you and he expect from its being published, in regard that it is so busy a time here in Parliament, and matters of so much importance there under debate, that were the sermon now in my lord Bishop's hand, I cannot expect his lordship's being at leisure to overlook it till some of those matters be passed, and our sitting in Parliament adjourned, which I suppose it may for some little time be at Christmas, which is now at hand. In which last consideration I do upon second thoughts think it best (for saving of time) to send it you back again without expecting your answer hereto, forasmuch as you may return it up to town again by the very next post, in case the author shall think fit to commit it to some friend here."

It is impossible to discuss Pepys the official without inquiring how far he was a corrupt official. During the period of the *Diary* his salary as Clerk of the Acts was £350 a year;[1] while in 1665 he was appointed Treasurer for the Tangier Commission, and from 1665 to 1667 he was Surveyor-General of Victualling at £300 a year. But these legitimate emoluments were supplemented in other ways. Readers of the *Diary* will remember that on 2nd Feb. 1664, he received "a pair of gloves" for his wife "wrapt up in paper," which he "would not open, feeling it hard;" this phenomenon being due to the presence, presumably in the fingers, of "forty pieces in good gold." Sir William Warren, the timber-merchant, gave him many presents, and shewed himself "a most useful and thankful man,"[2] bringing him on one occasion £100 " in a bag," which Pepys " joyfully " carried home in a coach, Warren himself " expressly taking care that nobody might see this business done."[3] On one occasion money came in a paper which Pepys opened in the office, taking the precaution of " not looking into it till all the money was out, that I might say I saw no money in the paper if ever I should be questioned about it."[4]   His

---

[1] Until 1665 this was charged with £100 a year, paid to Pepys's predecessor in office (*Diary*, 9th Feb. 1665).

[2] *Diary*, 6th Feb. 1664-5.

[3] *Ibid.*, 16th Sept. 1664.

[4] *Ibid.*, 3rd April 1663.

gifts of plate included " a noble silver warming-
pan."[1]

As Secretary of the Admiralty Pepys, now presumably a man of some means,[2] enjoyed what
was then a handsome salary of £500, but this
was only for two periods amounting altogether to
ten years; yet he acquired a modest competence[3]
and was able to indulge the expensive tastes of
the collector. If the standards of the time are
taken into account, it seems probable that the
Secretary of the Admiralty, as well as the Clerk
of the Acts, sometimes accepted presents. On
the other hand the official letters, numbering
thousands, conspire to produce, by a series of
delicate impressions, the unshakeable conviction
that Pepys was immensely proud of the Navy
and keenly anxious for its efficiency and success.
We may therefore, I think, acquit him of cor-

---

[1] *Diary*, 1st Jan. 1669. The illustrations given in the text are
by no means an exhaustive list of the presents received by Pepys.
Other gifts of money and plate are recorded in the *Diary* (*e.g.* 5th
Jan., 2nd and 27th May, 3rd, 10th, and 22nd June, 18th and 21st
July 1664; 21st Mar. 1665; 21st and 24th Feb. 1668), and he
appears to have profited largely by his transactions with Gauden,
the victualler of the Navy (21st July 1664; 4th Feb. and 2nd Aug.
1667), with the victuallers for Tangier (16th July and 10th Sept.
1664; 16th Mar. 1665; 31st Oct. and 27th Dec. 1667), and with
Captain Cocke, a contractor for hemp (25th May, 27th June, 14th
Aug., and 10th Nov. 1666). He also made profits out of flags
(27th Nov. 1664; 28th Jan. 1665; 28th May 1669), prizes (17th
July and 14th Aug. 1667; 3rd Feb. 1668), and Tangier freights
(28th Nov. and 9th Dec. 1664; 29th Mar. 1665).

[2] As early as 31st May 1667 he was worth £6900 (*Diary*).

[3] Part of his estate consisted of a claim on the Crown of
£28,007, 2s. 1¼d., due on accounts connected with his offices, but
this was never paid to his executors (Wheatley, *Pepysiana*, p. 51).

ruption in its grosser forms. His fundamental Puritanism affects him here also, and even in the *Diary* days he is always trying to justify to himself the presents which he accepted. He was glad to do the giver a good turn when he could, but it was with the proviso that it should be " without wrong to the king's service."[1] The author of this phrase is on dangerous ground, but he is not yet utterly debased ; and the high responsibility of later life may very well have been an antiseptic to arrest corruption even if it did not destroy it. At any rate there is no direct evidence of corruption to be found in the Pepysian documents at Cambridge, unless it be in the undeciphered shorthand notes on abuses contained in the *Navy White Book* ; but those are more likely to consist of caustic comments upon the shortcomings of other people.

It must be remembered that the name of Pepys carried great weight in the Navy during the century that succeeded his administration. The commission which reported in June, 1805, spoke of him as " a man of extraordinary knowledge in all that related to the business" of the Navy, " of great talents, and the most indefatigable industry ; "[2] and his tenure of office left a durable tradition of his greatness. The prodigious respect paid to his authority

---

[1] *Diary*, 10th Dec. 1663. Cf. *Ibid.*, 5th Jan., 10th and 24th Sept., 8th and 12th Oct. 1664, where the same mental attitude is indicated.

[2] *Historical MSS. Commission,* 15*th Report,* Appendix, pt. ii. p. 153.

F

by the naval administrators of the next generation
—comparable only perhaps to the weight which
Lord Chief Justice Coke had carried among the
lawyers of an earlier time—led to a number of trans-
cripts being made from the Pepysian MSS. and
preserved among the records of the Admiralty.

We may say that in a sense the worst enemy of
Pepys the official is Pepys the diarist ; and there
is a danger lest the intimate self-revelation of his
earlier life should be suffered to eclipse the record
of a fine career of public service. Yet, if viewed
as a whole, his career is indeed remarkable. It
is extraordinary that a man should have written
the *Diary*, but it is much more extraordinary
that the man who wrote the *Diary* should also
have been the right hand of the Navy. From
the *Diary* we learn that Pepys was a musician,
a dandy, a collector of books and prints, a man
of science, an observer of boundless curiosity,
and, as a critic has pointed out, one who possessed an " amazing zest for life." From the
Pepysian manuscripts we learn that he was a
man of sound judgment, of orderly and methodical
business habits, of great administrative capacity
and energy ; and that he possessed extraordinary
shrewdness and tact in dealing with men. It is
the combination of all these qualities that is so
astonishing, and those who regard him as a literary
performer making sport for the leisure of later
generations do little justice to the real Pepys.

NAVAL HISTORY AND THE NECESSITY
OF A CATALOGUE OF SOURCES

BY LIEUTENANT ALFRED DEWAR, R.N. (retired)

THE naval officer lives close to the elemental
things of life. His ambition is to make history,
not to study it. He is a profound believer in
the practical, and unless history can be translated
into terms of his favourite cult he will continue
to regard it with indifference and suspicion.
And yet, our Navy, sovereign mistress of the
avenues of revictualment and reinforcement,
inherits a greater history than any other nation's,
and the marrow of a true doctrine lies hidden in
the despatches of our great admirals; but it lies
for the most part ensepulchred on dusty shelves,
and the naval officer confines himself to the
occasional and wholly uncritical perusal of some
small text-book. From 1860 to 1900, the key-
note of higher education in the Navy was a
child-like faith in mathematics, with the result
that, up to a few years ago, history remained
the Cinderella of naval sciences. This neglect
has had certain inevitable results. While unexampled attention has been given to things
material and mechanical, the study of the

wider aspects of strategy has been left to itself.

Great issues, mirrored in the past, rush down upon us, and their attendant problems remain unsolved because we nurse the idea that the study of our earlier struggles is useless, unproductive and out of date. History is regarded by the naval officer as a dead science. Trained in mathematics, a science which deals with quantity and ignores qualitative differences, he rarely looks beyond the horizon of technical study, and like John Roskruge, is of opinion that a sailor's ideas should go no further than the jib-boom end.[1] The peculiar virtue once supposed to reside in mathematics is now ascribed to engineering, a science wholly wrapped up in things material and seriously defective as an educational instrument. Never dealing with abstract problems, engineering alone can never provide a complete education; and in fact there is something complementary between it and history, the former dealing with inert matter in the present, the latter with living entities and events in the past. Too much time in the engine-room produces what may be termed the " ironmonger's " mind, a mind trained to think in terms of matter and unable to deal with the sudden

---

[1] " John Roskruge, master, a good man ; better acquainted with ropeyarns and bilgewater than with Homer or Vergil. He said a man's ideas should go no further than the jibboom end." Recollections of James Anthony Gardner (N.R.S.), 91.

vicissitudes of political and worldly events. The disciples of engineering believe their science to be the science of war. But this is no more the case than in the past. The progress in the arts and crafts of war has increased the intensity of battle, but it has not altered the fundamental principles of strategy. The "science of war" in the words of one of its greatest practical exponents is the "history of war." "No living science can found itself on the present alone. Such an attitude hides deep in itself the seeds of bias, dogmatism and mental decay."[1]

At the same time the value of history must not be exaggerated. In the discussion on Colonel Maurice's paper an officer insisted that military history must be written in sufficient detail to assist the company commander. But the object of naval history is not to teach a lieutenant how to handle his boat; for the younger officer, mother wit, and a knowledge of his men and of his weapons, are sufficient. It is later that the value of history in dealing with larger problems asserts itself, but unless an officer begins its study when young he will have no time to master its craft when older. The remedy for the neglect of history in naval education lies not in text-books, but in bringing the mature mind directly into contact with the actual thought and opinions of the great masters of naval warfare in the past. It will

[1] Rosenberger, *Geschichte der Physik*, III., vi.

then be found that nursed in the same school,
confronted with the same problems, the naval
officer can interpret the ideas of his great pre-
decessors more skilfully than the civilian. As
he reads the letters of Lord Barham written
during the stress and strain of war, and hammered
into shape by the importunate violence of events,
he begins to see something beyond the pentagram
of routine and drill. The thin treble of manœuvres
gives place to the deep bass note of war. His
mind becomes attuned to general principles, and
the devitalising effect of purely technical study
is transformed and vivified in the alembic of the
past. But if the naval officer's conception of
history is at fault, the naval historian must bear
the larger portion of the blame. His work is too
often divorced from naval strategy, or as in James'
case tends to degenerate into a mere narrative
of battles.[1] The battle is merely the ultimate
potential strength at the moment of contact, and

[1] James is a conscientious writer and contains a great mass
of useful information, but his attention was focussed chiefly on
battles. He is lacking in a circumferential view of the main
problems of the period, rarely mentions his authorities, and as
he had no opportunity of consulting the instructions issued to
admirals, had to confine himself to a mere narrative of events.
He usually introduces frigate action by merely stating that on
a certain date an English frigate was in a certain place. But
what the naval officers want to know is the general distribution
of cruisers for commerce defence—for example, Middleton to
Pringle, Dec. 4, 1759; Barham Papers by Sir John Laughton
(Naval Records Society, i. 8); Admiral Philip Patton to Lord
Barham on cruiser distribution, June 27, 1794 (*ib.*, ii. 394).
Mahan, again, is rich in strategical criticism but rears his

casts no light on the strategy leading up to it. Again, each section of a campaign must be treated as a complete whole and must not be cut up into major and minor operations. The great majority of actions in defence of trade are minor actions, but the defence of trade is a major operation of the first importance. If naval history is to follow the path of the great schools of history at home and abroad, it must firstly be conversant with naval needs, and secondly must be in close touch with the thought and opinions of the great admirals of the past. In the great military nations military history receives a large meed of honour. But in our own pre-eminently naval nation it has for forty years been regarded as an academic and useless study. Such an idea is the infallible indication of the narrow-minded man who prefers to lodge like the gipsy in a rude tent pitched daily for the emergencies of the moment; one hates instinctively the firmer and nobler constructions of the historian.

But if we are to study history at its sources some guide to sources is absolutely necessary. We are the inheritors of a wealth of naval material unequalled in the annals of the world. But though the harvest is plenteous, the labourers are few. Three steps are required to render our

historical structure on a slender basis of authority ; his " Influence of Sea Power " is based wholly on secondary authorities, some of them (such as Lapeyrouse-Bonfils) of doubtful value.

naval archives accessible; firstly, a rough guide to sources; secondly, a catalogue for each source; thirdly, a Critical Catalogue[1] or Calendar.

Between the history of a contemporary war and of a war in the past, a great gulf is fixed. The discovery and collation of the materials of past history is really a craft in itself; and the historian of the past must reconstruct the life and movement of the period as a complete whole, to avoid falling into all sorts of hidden pitfalls.[2]

The preparation of a rough guide to sources does not offer any serious difficulties, and the accompanying pamphlet hurriedly compiled to accompany this paper is a specimen of one. The next requirement is a catalogue of each source, giving, for every paper of importance, the name of the writer, the date and the subject. The catalogue of Pepysian papers in the Rawlinson MSS. in the Bodleian is a good example of this kind; that of the British Museum is in some cases

[1] For a description of the critical catalogue or *Catalogue raisonnée* see Professor Firth's report in the Royal Commission on Public Records, 1912, vol. i. part ii. 103, 104. "For the cost of half a dozen volumes of the present calendar (*i.e.* State Papers Foreign) we could have a serviceable guide to the whole of the foreign State papers in the Record Office." With regard to the Calendar, Professor Firth says, "Were all records calendared, it would merely be the substitution of an unfathomable sea of print for an unfathomable see of manuscript."

[2] For instance, in Stenzel's *Seekriegsgeschichte*, a work well arranged on staff lines, the influence of Cromwell on the naval affairs of the Commonwealth is grossly exaggerated. See Vol. iii. 27, 31, 38.

NEED OF A CATALOGUE OF SOURCES 89

too vague to be of real assistance. In the case of the Record Office, where the great bulk of Admiralty papers and despatches are to be found, no catalogue of this sort exists, though its compilation for the more important sections (such as Admirals' Despatches) is well within the capacities of the card system. The List and Index[1] is the only guide available, but this (like some of the items in the British Museum Catalogues) only deals with parcels in bulk. It is simply a chronological guide, telling us that there are papers for a certain year respecting a certain fleet, and in some cases such as " Lords' Letters "[2] the headings convey no signification of the correspondence.

Lists and Indexes are, however, a comparatively recent publication. For many years the Record Office has been issuing Calendars[3] which aim at reproducing, partly or in full, documents which may be of value. Of these Calendars the State Papers Domestic started about 1856 are the principal example, and so far as they go (that is to 1695) contain a great deal of naval matter.[4]

[1] Lists and Indexes, Public Record Office, no. xviii., *Admiralty Papers*, vol. i., 1904.

[2] See Mr Julian Corbett's evidence before the Records Commission (Report of Royal Commission, 1912, vol. i. part iii. 89) ; also Sir John Laughton's, 74, and Mr W. G. Perrin's, 95.

[3] See Record Office publications, List F.

[4] There are few papers of any value in the Admiralty Records previous to 1660 ; the State Papers Domestic are therefore the principal source for the reigns of James I., Charles I., and the Interregnum.

But to quote Mr Paul Meyer, " these calendars
are interminable." [1]   They reverse the fable of
Achilles and the tortoise.   It is Achilles at the
present moment who flies ; it is the tortoise in the
form of a Calendar which pursues.   The Calendar
of State Papers Domestic has reached the year 1695,
and it has taken forty-three years to compile ninety-
five years of the seventeenth century.   Its value,
too, for naval purposes is greatly diminished after
1673,[2] at which year the compilers of the Calendar
began to reduce the naval matter inserted.

The naval material in these calendars, however,
is only there as part of the State Papers Domestic,
and has no connection with the Admiralty records,
none of which have yet been calendared.   The
principal calendars of strictly naval papers are to
be found in the Naval Records Society,[3] of which
Dr Tanner's Descriptive Catalogue of Pepysian
MSS. is an example.   But how slowly such work
proceeds !   In ten years (1903-13) three volumes
have appeared, containing a Register of Sea
Officers, a Register of Ships, and the Admiralty
Letters in the Pepysian collection for 1673 to
1677.   The most valuable part of the work is
the general introduction (vol. i. 1-251), which

[1] *Public Records Commmission*, 1912, vol. i. pt. ii. 136.
[2] A peculiarly inopportune year right in the middle of a naval
war ; see Dr Frith, *Public Records Com.*, vol. i. pt. iii. 75.
[3] Sir John Laughton's *Defeat of Spanish Armada*, 1894, 2 vols.,
Admiral Sturges Jackson's *Logs of the Great Sea Fights*, 2 vols.,
1899.   John Leyland's *Blockade of Brest*, 1898.   But note that
these calendars are all compiled round some central topic.

constitutes a history of naval administration from 1660 to 1688. With regard to the remainder, while the scholarship of the work is unquestionable, it is doubtful whether the actual reproduction of such documents as fill volume iii. is worth the time and energy involved; and in this question we debouch on what may be called the controversy between the Calendar and the French system of critical catalogues. To calendar papers without some definite and important problem to act as a winnowing fan leads to a great deal of waste material. The numerous volumes of the first Calendar of Treasury Papers (1557-1728) are an instance of this, and another is the Calendar of the Committee for the Advance of Money and the Calendar of the Committee for Compounding— two committees for raising money from delinquents in Commonwealth times. These bulky volumes give a great deal of genealogical[1] information, but make no mention of the total sum raised by this means, the first question which rises in the mind of anyone interested in the finance of the period. Just as, in the Navy, paint-work sometimes usurps the place of gunnery, so in the Calendars genealogy sometimes takes the place of finance. Now, if a Calendar is badly compiled, the mistake is almost irremediable.

---

[1] Compare Mr Julian Corbett's evidence, *Public Records Commission*, vol. i. part iii. q. 2505. "There is an air of family history over the whole Record Office."

In France, however, what may be called the final finger-post to sources is not a Calendar but a critical catalogue, of which the *Inventaire Sommaire* series is an example. Each volume of records is briefly criticised in half a page or page of the *Sommaire*. In this system a very definite index to sources can be supplied in a reasonable time and can be easily amended and supplemented.

It seems certain, however, that any attempt to deal in this way with the untouched accumulation of centuries must be done on a collective basis, but this very necessity gives us the desired opportunity of bringing the naval officer in touch with sources.

We must first decide what are the most important sections of the Admiralty records. This presents no difficulty. There are three principal sections, In-Letters, Out-Letters and Admiralty Minutes. Of the In-Letters, Admirals' Despatches, Secret Letters and Courts Martial are the more important : of the Out-Letters, Orders and Instructions. These require to be precisely catalogued for all periods of war. As the Admirals' Despatches are arranged, conveniently enough, according to stations, there would be no great difficulty in this. At first the mass of stuff appears somewhat appalling, but if reduced to a single war it presents a more manageable form. Thus there are 1434 volumes of Admirals' Despatches, but only 71 for the American War of Independence (1776-1783). The compilation of a simple catalogue of these despatches, giving the date, writer, and subject would be a merely mechanical task,[1] and the catalogue would be equally useful whether we were studying a campaign or the history of a subject such as Commerce, Protection, or Invasion. The next step, the preparation of a *Catalogue raisonnée* or critical catalogue, requires a historical knowledge of the period and its problems. But what is the object of our staff course for officers if it cannot surmount this difficulty ? The staff course should take up a campaign or subject for the year. The main outlines, the controversial points, would first be sketched in half a dozen lectures by the historian in charge, and the attention of the class focussed rather on what is *not* known than on what is known about the war. Nor would this work be so extensive as it at first appears, for in any campaign there are certain days, weeks, months when the intensity of war approaches a maximum, and these are the periods on which attention requires to be focussed and the movement of almost every gunboat noted.

Last of all, there is a point where great economy of time and effort could be gained. If the

[1] See estimate of time by card system in similar case suggested by Mr W. P. Baildon, F.S.A., *Public Records Com.*, vol. i. pt. iii. 150.

Admiralty were definitely to take charge of the work and throw their ægis over it, it could be done much more quickly and economically. For the Admiralty has large powers of borrowing its own records,[1] and it would be possible for them to borrow thirty or forty volumes of Admirals' Despatches at a time and have them carded and criticised under proper supervision in the Admiralty Library, where the work would be done more conveniently than in the Record Office. Some such basis of collective effort must be adopted if our great wealth of sources is to be opened up, and at the same time brought into touch with the naval officer. But whatever method be employed, whether we use Calendars or critical catalogues, whether we write the history of a campaign, or trace out the evolution of some dominant feature of naval strategy, one thing remains certain—" Things can only be rightly understood by studying their origin,"—" Eine Sache wird nur völlig auf dem Wege verstanden wie sie selbst entsteht ; in dem genetischen Verfahren sind die Gründe der Sache auch die Gründe des Erkennens."[2] The science of war is the history of war, and history roughly understood is the expression of man's faith in

[1] *Public Records Commission*, Appendix, viii., on Relations of P.R.O. with Departments, vol. i. pt. ii. 115. See also Sir Maxwell Lyte's evidence, vol. i. pt. iii. 17.

[2] Trendelenburg, *Logische Untersuchungen*, ii. 388, 395. Acton's *Study of History*, 77.

the ultimate victory of Truth, just as Law is the expression of his faith in divine Justice.

APPENDIX

ROUGH GUIDE TO BRITISH SOURCES OF NAVAL HISTORY IN THE SEVENTEENTH CENTURY

I. NAVAL HISTORIES.

II. HISTORICAL ARTICLES IN REVIEWS AND MAGAZINES.

III. BIOGRAPHICAL.

IV. CONTEMPORARY WORKS—(a) NAVAL, (b) TECHNICAL.

V. PAMPHLETS.

VI. STATE PAPERS AND RECORD OFFICE.

VII. MSS. AT BRITISH MUSEUM, PEPYSIAN LIBRARY, BODLEIAN, AND ELSEWHERE.

VIII. HISTORICAL MSS. COMMISSION.

IX. PARLIAMENTARY JOURNALS, STATUTES, AND NEWS-LETTERS.

X. TOPOGRAPHY AND PORTRAITURE.

XI. SOME DUTCH AND FRENCH BOOKS.

96   NAVAL ESSAYS

I. NAVAL HISTORIES

*The asterisks indicate the principal works.

*BURCHETT'S NAVAL HISTORY. Josiah Burchett, Secretary to Admiralty, folio, 1720. (An authority for 1688 to 1712.)

COLUMNA ROSTRATA. S. Colliber, 1727. (Useful for Dutch Wars.)

LEDIARD'S NAVAL HISTORY. Thos. Lediard, 2 vols., folio, 1735. (Useful for comparison and gives authorities.)

ENTINCK'S NAVAL HISTORY. John Entinck, 1757 (gives authorities).

HISTORY OF MARINE ARCHITECTURE. John Charnock. 3 vols., 1800-02. (Interesting lists.)

NAVAL COMMISSIONERS FROM 1660 TO 1760. Sir George Jackson, 1889. (Privately printed.)

INFLUENCE OF SEA POWER ON HISTORY. Captain A. T. Mahan. Chapter I. can be read with benefit. The chapters on seventeenth century Naval History have been superseded by later writers, 1889.

NAVAL WARFARE. Vice-Admiral P. H. Colomb, 2nd edition, 1895. (An instructive book.)

*ROYAL NAVY FROM EARLIEST TIMES. W. Laird Clowes, 7 vols., 1898. (Vol. II. deals with seventeenth century to 1660 by L. Carr Laughton, from 1660 by Laird Clowes. Very useful but heavy, and no bibliography; and arrangement into major and minor operations open to criticism.)

*SHORT HISTORY OF ROYAL NAVY. D. Hannay, 2 vols., 1898. (Vol. I., 1213-1688—a useful handbook.)

*ENGLAND IN THE MEDITERRANEAN, 1603-1714. Julian Corbett, 2 vols., 1904. (Interesting and stimulative on navy of James I. and Commonwealth, and naval strategy in Mediterranean.)

*FIGHTING INSTRUCTIONS. 1530-1816. Julian Corbett, Naval Records Society, 1905. (The evolution of tactics and instructions for fighting.)

*ADMINISTRATION OF ROYAL NAVY FROM 1509 TO 1660. M. Oppenheim, 1906. Vol. I. (no second volume issued). (An indispensable book, full of information and figures.)

*NAVY OF COMMONWEALTH AND FIRST DUTCH WAR. J. R. Tanner. Camb. Mod. Hist., IV., 1906.

*ANGLO-DUTCH WARS. J. R. Tanner and C. T. Atkinson, Camb. Mod. Hist., V., 1908. (The best monographs on the Dutch Wars.)

THE DARTMOUTH DRAWINGS OF SOLEBAY (1672) AND TEXEL (1673). Julian Corbett (N.R.S., 1908).

ANGLO-DUTCH RIVALRY. George Edmundson, 1911.

[Gardiner's History of England, and Firth's Protectorate contain much naval matter.]

II. ARTICLES IN REVIEWS AND MAGAZINES

NATIONAL FLAGS OF THE COMMONWEALTH. Journal British Arch. Assoc., XXXI., 1875.

BATTLE OF LA HOGUE, 1692. Correspondence of Sir Wm. Haddock, Camden Miscellany, Vol. VIII., 1883.

ADMINISTRATION OF NAVY FROM RESTORATION TO REVOLUTION. J. R. Tanner, Eng. Hist. Review, Vols. XII., XIII., XIV., 1897-99.

BLAKE AND BATTLE OF ST CRUZ. C. H. Firth, English Hist. Review, April 1905. (The only correct account of Blake's battle at St Cruz.)

BLAKE'S LAST CAMPAIGN (1656-57). United Service Magazine, May 1911. (The only printed list of Blake's Fleet in 1656-57.)

[There must be many hundreds of others, and a complete list of articles *based on sources and giving references* is greatly wanted.]

III. BIOGRAPHICAL

Life of General Monk. Thomas Gumble, 1671.

Life and Glorious Actions of Sir George Rooke, 1707.

Robert Blake, Life of, by a gentleman bred in his family. (Date about 1716. Chiefly on authority of Mr Thomas Bear, who had served with Blake. Some gross inaccuracies, but accounts of battles are correct.)

Life of General Monk. T. Skinner, W. Webster, 1723.

Life of Sir John Leake. Stephen Martin Leake, 1750.

Biographia Navalis. John Charnock, 4 vols., 1794, and 2 vols. continuation. Portraits by Bartolozzi. (Begins 1660: Vol. I., 1660-73 ; II., 1674-91 ; III., 1693-1707.)

*Lives of the British Admirals. J. Campbell, 4 vols., 1774—, 1779, 8 vols., 1812. (Second vol. deals with Blake, Monk, Montague, Rupert, Lawson, Ayscue, Spragge, Kempthorne, etc.)

*Memoirs of Sir William Penn, by Granville Penn, 2 vols., 1833. (Contains many papers on Civil and Dutch Wars.)

Memoirs of Prince Rupert. Eliot Warburton, 3 vols., 1849.

Robert Blake. Hepworth Dixon, 1852. (Not very good.)

Life of Richard Deane, General at Sea. J. B. Deane, 1870.

Life of Admiral Robert Fairfax. Sir Clements Markham, 1884. (Period 1666-1725, at capture of Gibraltar.)

*Life of Monk. Julian Corbett, 1885.

*Robert Blake. David Hannay, 1886.

*Memoirs of Lord Torrington (1681-1733). Sir J. K. Laughton, Camden Society, 1889.

Life of Richard Badiley. J. A. Spalding, 1899.

Life of Captain Stephen Martin (1688-1715). Clements Markham, N.R.S., 1905.

APPENDIX 99

*LIFE OF MONTAGU, Earl of Sandwich. F. R. Harris, 2 vols., 1912.

*DICTIONARY OF NATIONAL BIOGRAPHY. Articles by Sir John Laughton. (Allen, Coventry, Holmes, Lawson, Penn, etc.)

IV. CONTEMPORARY WORKS—(a) NAVAL

JUDICIOUS AND SELECT ESSAYS AND OBSERVATIONS ON THE NAVY. Sir Walter Raleigh, 1650.

WORKS OF SIR WALTER RALEIGH, 8 vols., Oxford, 1829.

1625 VOYAGE TO CADIZ IN 1625. Journal of John Glanville. (A. B. Grosart, Camden Soc., 1883.)

JOURNAL OF EXPEDITION TO CADIZ in Works of George, Lord Lansdowne, 1736, Vol. III.

1627 EXPEDITION TO THE ISLE OF RHÉ. Herbert, Lord Cherbury. (Lord Powis, Philobiblon Society, 1860.)

1628 JOURNAL OF A VOYAGE TO THE MEDITERRANEAN. Sir Kenelm Digby, 1628. (J. Bruce, Camden Soc., 1868.)

1633 SOVEREIGNTY OF THE BRITISH SEAS. Sir John Borough, 1651.

1635 DIALLOGICAL DISCOURSE. Nathaniel Boteler. (Partly printed, 1685.)

1637 TRUE JOURNAL OF THE SALLEE FLEET. John Dunton, 1637.

1638. Thos. HEYWOOD (see (b) Technical).

1638 DISCOURSE ON THE NAVY, by John Holland, 1638-1659. J. R. Tanner, Naval Records Society, 1906. (Very valuable for victualling, pay, stores.)

1652-54 LETTERS AND PAPERS OF THE FIRST DUTCH WAR. S. R. Gardiner and C. T. Atkinson, Navy Record Society, 5 vols., issued 1899-1902. (An exhaustive compilation of all State Papers, Pamphlets, Newsletters and MSS. relating to the War, with the journals of the Dutch Admirals from the Hague.)

1654-55 NARRATIVE OF GENERAL VENABLES relating to the Expedition to the West Indies, 1654-55. C. H. Firth, Royal Hist. Soc., 1900.

1660 DISCOURSE ON THE NAVY. Sir Robert Slingsby. (With Holland's Discourse, J. R. Tanner, N.R.S., 1906.)

1660-67 DIARY OF SAMUEL PEPYS. Henry B. Wheatley, 9 vols., 1893-99. (The fullest and best edition ; also Pepysiana, by the same.)

1673 MEMOIRS OF ENGLISH AFFAIRS, chiefly Naval (1670-1673) by H.R.H. James, Duke of York, 1729. (A collection of Naval Orders.)

1675-79 DIARY OF HENRY TEONGE, Chaplain to the " Assistance," " Bristol," and " Royal Oak," 1675-79. 1825, editor unknown, vide Mariner's Mirror, June 1912, and notes by Sir J. Laughton in August 1912. The MS. seems to have been extant in 1887.

1688 MEMOIRS relating to the State of the Navy for Ten Years (1678-88). S. Pepys, London, 1690. (New edition, J. R. Tanner, Oxford, 1906.)

1694 JOURNAL OF BREST EXPEDITION. Marquis of Caermarthen, 1694.

1697 MEMOIRS OF TRANSACTIONS AT SEA DURING THE WAR WITH FRANCE, 1688-97. Josiah Burchett, 1703. (Secretary to Admiralty, 1695 ; an authority for period 1688-1709.)

1702 REFLECTIONS ON MR BURCHETT'S MEMOIRS, by Colonel Lillingston, 1704. (Deals with West Indies.)

1702 JOURNAL OF SIR GEORGE ROOKE. Oscar Browning, N.R.S., 1897.

1703 DISCOURSE OF THE MEDITERRANEAN SEA AND STRAITS OF GIBRALTAR. Sir Henry Sheeres, 1703. (Writer had much to do with Tangier.)

The following volumes of the Hakluyt Society refer to the seventeenth century :—

27. 1607-13.	82, 83. Java, 1690-98.
56. East Indies.	Second Series, 12, Bengal.
57. Hawkins' Voyages.	16. East Indies, 1608-17.
63. 1612-22.	17. Travels, Europe, 1808-1828.
66, 67. Japan, 1615-22.	87. Levant, 1600, 1670-79.
74, 75. Bengal, 1681-87.	88, 89, 96, 97. North-West
79. Tractatus de globis.	Passages.

The following contain naval matter :—

SIR W. TEMPLE, LETTERS, 1665-72, 3 vols., 1702-3.

WORKS OF JOHN SHEFFIELD, DUKE OF BUCKINGHAM, 1729. (Went to sea as a volunteer in Second Dutch War.)

COMTE D'ESTRADES, LETTRES ET MEMOIRES, 9 vols., London, 1743.

SIR W. TEMPLE, WORKS OF, 4 vols., 1814.

LIFE OF CLARENDON, 3 vols., Oxford, 1827. See Lecture on Edward Hyde, Earl of Clarendon. C. H. Firth, 1909.

HISTORY OF MY OWN TIMES, Gilbert Burnet, 6 vols., 1833. See also Supplement by Foxcroft.

WHITELOCKE'S MEMOIRS, 4 vols., 1853. (Mentions all captures made.)

SWEDISH EMBASSY OF BULSTRODE WHITELOCKE. Henry Reeve, 1855.

CONTEMPORARY WORKS—(b) TECHNICAL

1613 ABRIDGMENT OF ALL SEA TERMES. William Wellwood, 1613.

*1625 SEAMAN'S DICTIONARY. Sir Henry Mainwaring, 1644. (See Oppenheim's Administration, 208.)

*1627 SEA GRAMMAR. Capt. John Smith, 1627.

*1629 ARCHITECTURA NAVALIS. Jo. Furtenbach, 1629.

1636 THE NAVIGATOR. Chas. Salstonstall, 1636.

*1638　TRUE DESCRIPTION OF A SHIP CALLED "THE SOVE-
　　　　REIGN OF THE SEA." Thos. Heywood, 1638.

　1644　PATHWAY TO PERFECT SAILING. Richard Polter,
　　　　1644.

*1644　NAVIUM FIGURAE. W. Hollar, 12 plates of ships,
　　　　1647.

　1660　SIZE AND LENGTH OF RIGGING FOR ALL SHIPS.
　　　　E. Hayward, folio, 1660.

　1664　THE BOATSWAIN'S ART, OR THE COMPLETE BOAT-
　　　　SWAIN. Henry Bond, 1664.

　1664　THE COMPLETE SHIPWRIGHT. Edmund Bushnell,
　　　　1664. Later editions, 1669, 1678.

　1671　SCHIEPSBOUW. NICOLAS WITSEN, folio, Amsterdam,
　　　　1671.

　1691　NIEDERLANDSCHE SCHIEPSBOUWKONST. Cornelius
　　　　van Yk., folio, 1677.

V. PAMPHLETS

The Catalogue of Thomason Tracts (in British Museum)
should be consulted.

The following are a selection, omitting the numerous
pamphlets on engagements, of which there are 29 for the First
Dutch War alone in the Thomason Collection :—

　1645　BURRELL'S ANSWERS TO QUESTIONS OF THE COM-
　　　　MITTEE OF THE HOUSE OF COMMONS, 1645.

　1647　A DECLARATION IN VINDICATION OF THE HOUSES OF
　　　　PARLIAMENT AND OF THE COMMITTEE OF THE NAVY
　　　　AND CUSTOMS. Giles Greene. (Greene was a member
　　　　of the Navy Committee ; contains interesting figures.)

　1648　DECLARATION OF EARL OF WARWICK, 1648.
　　　　　DECLARATION OF HIS EXCELLENCY THE EARL OF
　　　　　　WARWICK, 1648.
　　　　　" PERFECT REMONSTRANCE " OF THE EARL OF
　　　　　　WARWICK, 1648.

　1656　ANSWER OF THE COMMISSIONERS OF THE NAVY TO A
　　　　SCANDALOUS PAMPHLET BY MR ANDREW BURRELLS,
　　　　1656, 30 pages.

1664 BRIEF RELATION OF THE PRESENT STATE OF TANGIER, 1664.

1689 OBSERVATIONS CONCERNING DOMINION AND SOVE-REIGNTY OF THE SEA. Sir Philip Meadows, 1689, 47 pages.

1691 NAVAL SPECULATIONS AND MARITIME POLITICS. Henry Maydman, 1691. (A criticism on the Navy; writer was a Purser under the Commonwealth, and Mayor of Portsmouth, 1710. Oppenheim's Administration, 350.)

1694 ENGLAND'S INTEREST. Capt. Yeo St Lo, 1694, 51 pages. (Impressment and manning.)

1695 GREAT BRITAIN'S TEARS. Robert Crossfield, 1695, 16 pages. (Grievances of seamen.)

1695 JUSTICE PERVERTED AND INNOCENCE OPPRESSED. Robert Crossfield, 1695, 31 pages. (Corrupt practices of dockyards.)

1695 GREAT BRITAIN'S GRIEVANCES. W. Hodges, 1695, 26 pages. (Ticket System, etc.)

1695 JOURNAL OF VICTORIOUS EXPEDITION UNDER ADMIRAL RUSSELL, 1695, 28 pages. (Relief of Barcelona, April, 1694-95.)

1700 REMARKS UPON THE NAVY. Letter from a Sailor to a Member of Parliament, 1700, 30 pages. (Discipline and grievances.)

1702 PRESENT CONDITION OF ENGLISH NAVY. A Dialogue between Young Fudge and Captain Steerwell, an Oliverian Commander. 1702, 32 pages. [The Oliverian Commander says, "For my part I never saw fighting in line. We never used it" (the line).]

1703 HISTORICAL AND POLITICAL TREATISE OF THE NAVY, 1703, 32 pages.

Many other pamphlets, numbering about a hundred, and including a great many accounts of engagements in the Dutch Wars: "A Bloody Fight"; "Another Bloody Fight"; "A more perfect Relation", etc., for almost every battle that took place, and for some that did not.

VI. STATE PAPERS AND RECORD OFFICE

The State Papers Domestic are nearly all calendared for the seventeenth century, in 67 volumes, from 1601 to 1695. There is a mass of naval information in the calendars up to 1673; and an abstract for any period, giving dates, senders and recipients of letters would be a sufficient guide to the original papers.

The Admiralty Papers in the Record Office are classified in the List of Admiralty Records, Vol. I. (Public Record Office, Lists and Indexes, No. XVIII., 1904).

Generally speaking, there are no papers in the Admiralty records previous to the Restoration (1660). There are nine main headings: Secretary's Department, Accountant General, Navy Board, Victualling, Marine Office, Medical, Controller, Transport, and Greenwich Hospital. The most important for the seventeenth century are the Secretary's and the Navy Board.

The headings of the Secretary's Department are In-Letters, Out-Letters, Minutes, Letters Patent, Registers, List Books, Officers' Services, Indexes and Digests, Miscellanea.

The In-Letters have 52 divisions, of which the most important are Admirals' Despatches, Port Admirals, Captains' Letters, Lieutenants' Letters, Minute Branch, Navy Board, Intelligence, Secretaries of State, and Courts Martial.

The Out-Letters have 23 divisions, of which the most important are Secret Orders, Orders and Instructions, Lords' Letters, and Secretary's Letters.

The sub-division of Admirals' Despatches is divided into 17 stations, and in each station the volumes form a chronological series. Thus the Channel Fleet begins at 1743-47; East Indies, 1744; Mediterranean, 1705. The earliest Port Admiral series is Sheerness, 1708. This classification makes it very difficult for one person to collate the material for a particular campaign.

The series Captains' Letters is divided on still more diverse lines, alphabetically according to the captains' names, and then chronologically, the earliest beginning in 1698. Letters from the Navy Board begin in 1673; from Secretaries of State, 1689; and Courts Martial are recorded from 1680.

The series Orders and Instructions of the Out-Letters begins in 1665, but 1679 to 1689 is missing. This is the earliest series in the Admiralty Papers at the Record Office.

VII. MSS., NAVAL

BRITISH MUSEUM, MAGDALENE, BODLEIAN

The principal collections of MSS. in the British Museum are the Cotton, Harleian (acquired 1753), Sloane (in 1752), Stowe and Additional MSS.

See Catalogue of Stowe MSS., 2 vols., Harleian MSS., 4 vols., and Additional MSS., 1905. Also Subject Catalogue of MSS. in MSS. Room.

Oppenheim quotes largely from British Museum MSS.

The following is a selection :—

MANSELL'S DISCOVERY OF HOLLAND'S TRADE OF FISHING AND THE CIRCUMVENTING OF THEM.

OBSERVATIONS ON COAL TRADE AT NEWCASTLE, 2623.

NOTES ON COAL TRADE, 4459. (Coal trade was one of the most important branches of trade in the seventeenth century.)

BOTELER'S DISCOURSE, 1635. Sloane, 2449, partly printed, 1685.

W. PENN'S NAVAL TRACTS, BRIEF DISCOURSE OF THE NAVY. Sloane, 3232.

R. GIBSON, PAPERS RELATING TO THE NAVY, 1650-1702. Add. MSS., 11602, 11684. (Gibson served during Commonwealth and First Dutch War, and then at Admiralty; mentioned several times in Pepys's Diary; some of his papers printed in Gardiner and Atkinson.)

PAPERS RELATING TO NAVY, 1611-1769. Add. MSS., 18772, 19029-35.

PAPERS RELATING TO THE NAVY OFFICE, 1644-99. Add MSS. 18986.

LETTERS RELATING TO NAVY, 1640-1718. Add. MSS., 19367.

NAVAL TRACTS. Add. MSS., 533.

WEALE'S JOURNAL. Sloane, 1431 (Blake in Mediterranean).

RUPERT'S CORRESPONDENCE. Add. MSS., 18980-2, 19098, 27790.

PAPERS OF SIR HENRY COVENTRY (Third Dutch War). Add. MSS., 32094.

HADDOCK PAPERS (Reign of William III. and Anne). Egerton, 2520-32.

LETTERS, SIR JOHN TRENCHARD, with Killigrew and Shovell, 1693. Add. MSS., 35855, 35898.

ORDERS AND JOURNALS OF MATTHEW AYLMER, 1690-99. Add. MSS., 28122-4.

PAPERS OF SIR GEORGE ROOKE. Add. MSS., 28125, 28925.

PAPERS OF ADMIRAL SIR JOHN NORRIS. Add. MSS., 28122, 28157.

PEPYSIAN LIBRARY AT MAGDALENE COLLEGE

The Pepysian Library at Cambridge contains some 120 volumes of Naval MSS., including—

ADMIRALTY LETTERS, 14 vols., from June 1673.

MISCELLANIES, 12 vols.

NAVAL MINUTES (2866).

REGISTER OF ROYAL NAVY SHIPS, 1660-86 (2940).

REGISTER OF SEA OFFICERS, 1660-88 (2941).

DIARY RELATING TO THE COMMISSION OF 1686 (1490).

KING JAMES' POCKET BOOK OF RATES AND MEMORANDA (488).

MEMOIRS RELATING TO THE STATE OF THE NAVY, 1678-88, printed 1690. (J. R. Tanner, Oxford, 1906.)

AN INQUISITION BY H.R.H. THE DUKE OF YORK INTO NAVAL AFFAIRS, 1668 (2242).

A DESCRIPTIVE CATALOGUE OF PEPYSIAN MSS., by J. R. Tanner, Naval Records Society (3 vols., issued 1903-1909), is of the nature of a calendar. Vol. I. contains a Preface, which is really a history of naval administration, 1660-88, based on the Pepysian MSS. ; the Register of Ships, 1660-86, in full, 52 pages; and the Register of Sea Officers, 1660-88, in full, 126 pages. Vols. II. and III. contain a précis of the Admiralty Letters, June 1673 to May 1677. There is no handy printed Catalogue corresponding to the Catalogue of the Rawlinson MSS. at the Bodleian, and some restrictions are placed on the examination of the MSS.

NAVAL MSS. AT THE BODLEIAN

The Rawlinson MSS. contain some 65 volumes of papers which belonged to Pepys, and about 17 volumes of the Thurloe Papers contain references to naval subjects. A few of the volumes of the Tanner MSS. contain some important naval letters for the Civil War and the First Dutch War.

The following is a rough guide : A,B,C,D, signify Rawlinson ; T signifies Tanner ; the numbers signify volumes in which the papers are to be found. See Catalogues of Rawlinson and Tanner MSS.

END OF SIXTEENTH CENTURY. A171, A192, Drawings of Cannon and Gunner's Arte, by Lad, C846.

SURVEY OF NAVY IN 1618. A192, A215, A455.

FROM 1618 TO 1642. A210, Account of Rochelle Expedition, 1627.

CIVIL WAR AND COMMONWEALTH. A223, Navy Estimates, 1642-54 ; A225, 226, 227, Letter Books of Admiralty Committee and Commissioners, October 28, 1650, to August 19, 1653 ; A207, Minute Book of Navy Commissioners, October 1650 to Jan. 1653 ; T56, Letters of Deane, Blake, and Monk (about 24) for 1652-53 ; T56, Half a dozen Letters, Blake, 1649 ; T57, Letters on Revolt of Fleet, 1648. (All the Tanner Letters for the First Dutch War, 1652-54, are in Gardiner and Atkinson.)

PROTECTORATE. A181, 187, 195, A26, Goodson's Instructions, 1655; A36, Blake's Fleet, 1656; A37, List of Ships in His Highness' Navy, 1656; A44, 57, Estimate of Jamaica Expedition, 1654; Carte MSS., 73; Letters from Capt. John Stoakes in Mediterranean, 1658; C381, Letters from Capt. Thos. Whetstone (Quarrel with Stoakes), 1658.

[There are 67 vols. of Thurloe Papers in the Rawlinson MSS. The most important are printed in Thurloe State Papers, 7 vols., folio, 1742, which contain many letters on the Navy, from 1654 to 1658. Some of Thurloe's Papers went to the British Museum.]

SECOND DUTCH WAR (1665-67). A174, A187, A195, Papers put up by Pepys for a Collection on the War; 212, Navy Accounts; 457, Pepys' Answer to the Enquiry on the War; 468, Sandwich and Bergen Expedition, D924.

The Clarendon Papers in the Bodleian should also be consulted, but many are still uncalendared.

THIRD DUTCH WAR. A185, Flag Officers' Accounts of Engagement of May 28, 1672; A187, 191, T42, T114, Engagements, June 1666, August 8, 9, 1666; T296, Admiral Allin's Journal, 1660.

ADMINISTRATION. A191 (Ticket System), 181, 192, Holland's Discourse of 1638; 181, Papers Relating to Enquiry in 1679; 214, Orders of King and Admiralty, 1673-1679; 465, Proposition on ill state of Navy, January 26, 1686; 465, Notes of S. Pepys for Discourse to King, December 31, 1685; 463, A Diallogical Discourse of Marine Affayres; 189, State of Navy, January 26, 1686.

TANGIERS. A great deal about Tangiers, much of it printed in Life and Journals of S. Pepys. John Smith, 2 vols., 1841. A190, 191, 196, C423, 859, D916.

LISTS OF OFFICERS. A181 (1679 and 1678); A186 (1660-88); 197 (1660-88).

LIST OF SHIPS. A197, General Register (1660-75).

YEAR 1688-89. A170, 171, 179, 186, 32 Letters to S. Pepys from Lord Dartmouth. (Several printed in Life and Journals.)

SIR JOHN NARBOROUGH. A189, C1972.

ARTHUR HERBERT. A228, Letters, 1672-83.

SIR GEORGE ROOKE. A450, 451.

INSTRUCTIONS. A185, For Officers and Men of War in 1619 ; A193, 462, Northumberland's Instructions, November 14, 1640 ; A466, Duke of York for Navy Office, 1661 ; A919, Duke of York for better ordering of the Fleet in Sailing, 1664-65, and Instructions for Fighting, 1664.

There are also at Greenwich Museum 2 vols. of Navy Accounts, 1637-44 (Oppenheim, Administration, 247).

For other MSS. see Hist. MSS. Commission.

VIII. HISTORICAL MANUSCRIPTS COMMISSION

This Commission for the examination of MSS. in private hands dates from 1869. The designation of the volumes is clumsy. In following notes ("XII., 7") means Twelfth Report, Seventh Appendix, but in later volumes this classification has been submerged. See List of Hist. MSS. Commission, H.M. Stationery Office.

The following is a division into periods :—

NAVY OF JAMES I. AND CHARLES I. ; Bath Papers (III.) ; Cowper (XII., 1) ; Northumberland (III.) ; Muncaster (X., 4) ; De la Warr (IV.) ; Leconfield (VI.)

COMMONWEALTH; Portland (XIII., Vols. I. and II.) ; Leybourne Popham (1899).

CHARLES II. ; Malet (V.) ; Dartmouth (XI., 5).

FOR 1688 and WILLIAM III. House of Lords, New Series, Vols. I. and II. ; Buccleugh (1903) ; Delaval (XIII.).

BATH (MARQUIS OF) (III., IV.) Expeditions, 1600, 1602 ; A Book on the Navy, 1600 ; Navy ript and ransackt, by John Holland to Duke of York, 193 pages ; Discourse of Navy, 1638 ; Letters on Naval Affairs, 1664-1665 ; Lawson's Journal, 1660-2 ; Papers, 1663, 1664, 1667 ; Actions in Second and Third Dutch Wars (Sir William Coventry).

COWPER PAPERS (XII., 1). John Coke's Papers, 1600-28 ; Commission of 1618.

NORTHUMBERLAND (DUKE OF) (III.). Papers of Algernon, Earl of Northumberland, 1636 ; Statement of Abuses, 1637 ; Tromp and Oquendo, 1639.

MUNCASTER (X., 4). Pennington's Journal for Summer Guards of 1633-34-35-36.

DE LA WARR (IV.) Cranfield Papers, Decay of Navy, 1621 ; Report of Commissioners, 1621. John Coke and Lionel Cranfield were two of the principal agents in the attempted reform of the Navy under James I.

LECONFIELD (VI.) Commission of 1618, Instructions of George, Duke of Buckingham, 35 pages ; Duties of an Admiral, 71 pages ; Raleigh's Discourse on Ships, an abstract of things belonging to a ship, 357 pages ; A Brief Discourse of the Navy, January 26, 1638 ; Description of Masts, Rigging, etc. ; Northumberland's Journal, May to October, 1636.

PORTLAND PAPERS, Vol. I. (XIII. Report). Blake, Popham, Deane in 1650 ; II., Penn's Papers, 1649-69, many printed in Memorials of Sir W. Penn ; III., Journal of Sir Francis Wheeler in West Indies, March 1692 to April 1693.

LEYBOURNE POPHAM (1899). Deane, Popham and Blake, 1649 ; Popham's Journal for August to November 1649 ; April to July 1650 ; April to August 1651.

MALET (V.). Letters of Rupert and Albemarle, 1665-6, and Notes by Coventry.

DARTMOUTH (XI., 5). Allin's Journal to Straits, July 1669 to November 1670 ; Tangier, 1678-1683 ; Series of Letters from Pepys, September to December 1688.

HOUSE OF LORDS MSS., New Series, Vol. I. Enquiry into Sir George Rooke's Movements and Naval Miscarriages, 1693-94. Contains a great mass of naval information (pp. 93-291).

Vol. II., A mass of information on trade and captures for 1695-96 ; Letters of E. Indies Co., Royal African Co., with reply of Admiralty on Disposition of Ships, and Sir George Rooke's Papers.

BUCCLEUGH (Vol. II., part 1, 1903). Correspondence of Shrewsbury with Russell and Rooke, 1694, 1695.

DELAVAL (XIII.) Some Letters of Captain George Delaval at the end of century.

ELIOT HODGKINS (XV., 2). Some Letters of Pepys, 1666-73, and one or two Naval Letters, 1653, 1656.

IX. PARLIAMENTARY JOURNALS, STATUTES

THE COMMONS' AND LORDS' JOURNALS contain a great deal of information for the period from 1642 to 1653. (No Lords' Journal, 1649-60.)

For ACTS OF PARLIAMENT consult Statutes at Large. (No Acts recorded 1642 to 1660.)

ACTS AND ORDINANCES OF THE INTERREGNUM. C. H. Firth and R. S. Rait, 3 vols., 1911.

For TREATIES. Dumont's Collection de Traités, 12 vols.

For FRENCH DIPLOMATIC SOURCES see Notes on Diplomatic Relations of England and France, 1603-88. Firth and Lomas, Oxford, 1906.

NEWSPAPERS AND NEWSLETTERS

Newsletters are not so fruitful a source of information as in later times.

For the principal newspapers see History of English Journalism, by J. B. Williams, 1908 (1641-63), and Catalogue of Thomason Collection (British Museum).

The Gazette begins in 1665, as the "Oxford Gazette."

LIFE OF SIR ROGER LESTRANGE. George Kitchin, 1913.

The principal newspapers at the time of the First Dutch War were The Weekly Intelligencer (Tuesdays) ; A Perfect Account (Wednesdays) ; Mercurius Politicus (Thursdays) ; Perfect Passages (Fridays).

Sir Joseph Williamson's Newsletters (W. D. Christie, Camden Society, 1874) contain a good deal of information about the Third Dutch War (1672-74).

X. TOPOGRAPHY AND PORTRAITURE

See Catalogue of Plans and Maps, British Museum, 2 vols., 1885. There is a good collection of old Atlases in the Royal United Service Institution.

THE MARINER'S MIRROR, 1588. Luke Wagenaar (41 Charts).

SEESPIEGEL. W. J. Blaeu, 1649 (Charts and sailing directions).

OGILVY'S BRITANNICA DEPICTA, 1670.

SPEED'S ATLAS, 1676. (Diagrams of roads and good maps of Barbadoes, Jamaica, and Bermuda.)

DE WIT'S ATLAS, Holland, 1690 (R.U.S.I.).

SANSON'S ATLAS, 1693 (R.U.S.I.).

CAMDEN'S BRITANNIA, 1695.

DESCRIPTIVE CATALOGUE OF WORKS OF W. HOLLAR, 1745.

CATALOGUES OF EXHIBITIONS OF NATIONAL PORTRAITS, 1866, 1867, 1868.

CATALOGUE OF NAVAL EXHIBITION, 1891.

DESCRIPTIVE CATALOGUE OF GREENWICH PORTRAITS, 1906.

CUST'S NAVAL PRINTS. Henry Parker, 1911.

CATALOGUE OF NAVAL PRINTS. T. H. Parker, 1912.

FOLIO VOLUME OF FORTIFICATIONS. Add. MSS., 16370-1.

THE NATIONAL PORTRAIT GALLERY. Lionel Cust, 2 vols.

THE SUTHERLAND COLLECTION in the Bodleian. 50 vols. (Attached to Clarendon and Burnet's History. Catalogue in 2 vols.)

LARGE DUTCH COLLECTION OF PRINTS AND PICTURES at Mauritzhuis, the Hague; Ryks Museum, Amsterdam; and Boyman's Museum, Rotterdam.

XI. SOME DUTCH AND FRENCH BOOKS

HET LEVEN VAN Z. JOHAN VAN GALEN. A. Montanus, 1653. Saken van Stael en Oorlogh. Lieuwe van Aitzema, 1669, 7 vols. fo. (full of information on foreign relations and proceedings of States General, but old print and clumsy).

LEVEN EN BEDRYF VAN MICHIEL DE RUITER. Gerard Brandt, folio, 1687, also 1732 and 1794.

LA VIE DE CORNEILLE TROMP. Hague, 1694.

LIFE OF CORNELIUS VAN TROMP. London, 1697 (Dutch sources).

L'ART DES ARMÉES NAVALES. Paul Hoste, 1697.

VIE DE RUYTER. French edition of above, 1698.

LEVEN EN DADEN DER DOORLUGTISTE ZEEHELDEN. L. v. d. Bos, 1683.

MÉMOIRES DU MARÉCHAL DE TOURVILLE. 3 vols., 1758.

—— Levens beschryving van Johan en Cornelis Evertsen, 1820.

LEVEN EN DADEN VAN MARTEN H. TROMP EN JACOB VAN WASSANAER VAN OBDAM. J. A. Oostkamp, 1825.

JONGE, J. C. de. Geschiedenis van het Nederlandsche Zeewezen, 6 vols., 1833-48.

HISTOIRE DE LA MARINE FRANÇAISE. Eugene Sue, 5 vols., 1835-37.

HISTOIRE MARITIME DE LA FRANCE. Leon Guerin, 2 vols., 1844.

DE NEDERLANDSCHE GESCHIEDENIS IN PLATEN. F. Muller, 1863, 4 vols. (Exhaustive account of Dutch historical prints.)

BATAILLES NAVALES. O. Troude, 1867.

LIFE OF JEAN DE WIT. A. Lefevre-Pontalis, Paris, 1884. (English Translation by S. Stephenson, 2 vols., 1885.)

HISTOIRE DE LA MARINE FRANÇAISE. C. de la Roncière (Vol. IV., 17th century), 1899-1906.

H

DE VERWISKELINGEN TUSSCHEN DE REPUBLEK EN ENGELAND,
1660-65. N. Japiske, 1900.

REPERTORIUM VOOR DE NEDERLANDSCHE KRYGSGESCHIEDENIS.
F. de Bas, Hague, 1905.

MARINE MILITAIRE SOUS LOUIS XV. ET LOUIS XIV.
G. Lacour Gayet, 1911, 2 vols.

L'ÉTAT DES INVENTAIRES SOMMAIRES. L. Pannier.

LES ARCHIVES DE L'HISTOIRE DE FRANCE. C. V. Langlois
and H. Stein.

CATALOGUES OF DUTCH PAMPHLETS—
Pamphlets at Royal Library, the Hague, by Dr W. P. C.
Knuttel, 1899-1910, 8 vols.; at Leiden University, by
L. D. Petil, 1882-84, 2 vols.; Historical Pamphlets, by
P. A. Tiele, 1856-61, 8 vols. (gives a list of about 9500
pamphlets).

MILITARY ESSAYS

THE DIFFICULTIES ENCOUNTERED IN COMPILING MILITARY HISTORY

BY COLONEL SIR LONSDALE HALE

The purpose of this paper is to put before you some of the difficulties encountered in compiling the branch of Military History which deals with campaigns, battles, and other operations in the field, difficulties as often as not insuperable.

And by the words " Military History " I do not mean only the larger works, such as those of Alison, Thiers, Lehautcourt, Hoenig, Fortescue, Oman, and others, but records of all kinds and sizes, such as the excellent monographs of the German General Staff (the Kriegsgeschichtliche Einzelschriften), and pamphlets ; in short, all records whatever of war operations.

The difficulties to which I have referred are, however, not very great if the history is intended for general reading only. It is when it is intended for professional readers that they are encountered almost *ab initio* ; and for soldiers this history is of ultra-importance and an absolute necessity. It is for the whole military profession, for the huge mass of men who have to do the fighting, that history has this importance ; and why ?

Look at the difference between learning to

be a soldier and learning to be, say, a physician or a surgeon. The future physician begins by standing beside his elder in a hospital ward; he sees and hears him diagnose the disease of a human patient, notices the symptoms, reads the prescriptions, and watches the effect of the treatment; or in the operating theatre he watches some operation and follows it in detail, and can even practise his hand on flesh and bone, so that when he starts as physician or surgeon on his own account he has already seen, and to a small extent has perhaps already taken part in actual and real war against pain and suffering.

But when soldiers go to take part in real war and to practise the profession of soldiering, but an insignificant few have ever seen one minute of real war; it exists in their imagination only, and they try hard to imagine what it is like. Yet the soldier who knows nothing of what lies before him, of what he has to expect and how to meet it, is a worthless soldier, however high or low his degree. And the only sources whence he can obtain this knowledge or whence it can be given to him by others are the written records of wars, campaigns, battles and operations which constitute Military History. And these written records must contain matter useful to each and every rank of soldiers, from commanders of armies down to men in the ranks. But if the record is confined to a bare statement of facts and incidents it will be of little value as a teacher of war, for it will afford but little instruction.

Every incident is an effect due to some cause or causes; and if we are to profit by or be warned by the incident, the cause or causes must be ascertained and be given in the record.

But the contents of these records, if they are not to be misleading, must be accurate, and if they are to be instructive they must be full and detailed.

What then are the difficulties which, as I have said, are sometimes encountered and are insurmountable in the compilation of the record ?

The first and initial difficulty lies in ascertaining what has actually taken place.

I do not mean the principal or leading events in any operation, but the lesser events which combine to constitute them. That a position or a village was captured, that cavalry made a successful charge, that a counter-attack was unsuccessful, may be beyond dispute, but the moment we attempt to analyse these several incidents we get into a maze of uncertainty. Neither is there any doubt as to the new and larger lessons of war that a campaign offers; in 1866 the superiority of the breech-loader to the muzzle-loader; in 1870 that of the long-ranging chassepot over the short-ranging German rifle; the value of artillery in mass ; the need for carefully arranged mobilisation and concentration : all these were obvious from the outset. It is rather what I may call the personal teaching of a war that is so elusive.

To those who read in their newspaper at their breakfast-table a vivid account of, say, a battle fought only a few hours before and described by a newspaper correspondent, this statement may seem strange ; but accurate or inaccurate as these accounts may be they are but the impressions of the observer, vary according to his powers of observation, and can hardly be regarded as Military History. They are the work of literary military impressionists.

And here I must interpose some remarks of a personal character. I am not about to put before you anything new or original. You will find most of it in Glynski or other writers ; but I accept their views because they are endorsed by my own experience, which is, I think, somewhat unique.

In 1870, just before Sedan, I became a garrison instructor, and the war was then the engrossing subject. Since that time my professional work has kept me in close touch with Military History, and during those forty-two years this war has been the main source whence I have drawn instruction for my brother soldiers. With them I have visited nearly all the scenes of real combat in France, Alsace and Lorraine, and always with one purpose in view ; we strove to learn on the spot the " How " and the " Why ", but we were dependent on the record available at the time. Officers who had taken part in the war gave me information from time to time. And please mark this; *pari passu*, during those forty-two years, have accumulated on my study bookshelves some 200 records of the war, from books to pamphlets. And the information I have been able to give to others during forty-two years has been in proportion to the growth of the record or the Military History of the war. During forty-two years I have from time to time had to modify my first impressions; so I ought to know something of the difficulties attending the compilation of the history of a war.

The difficulties I am dealing with are due to the deficiency of evidence, and the doubtful value of much of such evidence as is forthcoming.

First of all, take any incident of war, whether a battle, the capture of a convoy, or the surprise of outposts. There are always two parties to these quarrels, and in all quarrels we must hear both sides before arriving at a sound judgment on the facts, or on the case. A one-sided account is not likely to be exactly correct; and yet it is all that we can hope to get for a long time. Again, some of the chief actors may themselves have fallen in the strife, and their evidence lies buried with them.

Next, in civil life our most likely sources of

information as to some incident are those persons
who have taken part in it.   But the evidence
given by the actors themselves as to any incident of war in which they have taken part
has from the nature of the case to be accepted
with the greatest caution.   We all know how
difficult it is to note and to describe accurately
something of excitement we have witnessed ;
and soldiers in the excitement of battle, with
not only their own lives but the lives of others
in their hands, in the roar and hurly-burly of
war and the battle-field, are the poorest and most
unreliable of eye-witnesses.   The mind is in an
abnormal condition, sense of proportion gets
out of proper working, small things are exaggerated, larger matters overlooked ; at best the
horizon of observation is limited to the vicinity,
time and its duration get wrong ; a man thinks
he sees what he does not see, and he may not see
what is clear and plain before him.

A staff officer once told me :—

"At that unfortunate encounter, I was from a
point of vantage observing and noting what each
of a very few companies did.   Some time afterwards I was present when the company commanders were each narrating what had taken
place in his little bit of the battle-field.   Their
honesty and desire to speak the truth were above
suspicion, and yet I could not have believed
that the narratives I should have to hear would

differ so extraordinarily from what I myself had witnessed."

Of course, there are available the reports from the various grades of the Military Hierarchy. These will doubtless be correct as to the general incidents and the general course of events, but beyond this they will not go ; and they can never be exhaustive as to details ; moreover, danger and comradeship in danger make men in the field wondrous kind to each other, and public pillorying for mistakes is at a discount.

" There was one of my battalions that did not carry out my orders ", wrote to me a general who was not satisfied with an operation, " but ", even to me, his intimate friend, he added, " I am not going to tell you which battalion it was."

Still more will a commander of a regiment or a battalion, if he is worthy of his command, endeavour to hide from public contempt any shortcomings which those under his command, whose good name he values as his own, may on some occasion perhaps be guilty of in war.

And when in our seeking for facts we pass on to endeavouring to ascertain how and why it was that some fact or incident happened—the " why " and the " wherefore "—then we encounter difficulties indeed.

An army in the field may be regarded as a manufactory, the output of which is success in war ; it is run by a general manager, managers,

superintendents, foremen, and a crowd of
" hands " as is a civil manufactory, the output
of which is, say, cotton goods ; but whereas in
the civil manufactory every " hand " has his fixed,
almost mechanical task, and the failure of a foreman or a few " hands " would not seriously affect
the output, with the army manufactory there
is little purely mechanical work for the " hands " ;
how each does the work that falls to him must
influence the result, and it is quite possible that
the failure of a single foreman or a single " hand "
may convert the whole output from success to
entire failure.

I doubt that this is realised by civilians. The
failure of a " hand " may be not neglect of duty
but a mere mistake. In ordinary life we are all
liable to make mistakes, but whereas our mistakes
may be serious to ourselves but not to others,
the mistake of a single officer or soldier may be
fatal to the success of a whole operation.

True it is in war :—

> " For want of a nail the shoe was lost,
> For want of a shoe the horse was lost,
> For want of a horse the rider was lost,
> For want of a rider the message was lost,
> For want of a message the battle was lost."

But in any operation it is not one but many
nails that will be missing from many shoes ; and
for the compilation of records of full value there

must be long and untiring searching after the missing nails, some quite unfindable, and others perhaps by chance fitting some shoe to which they do not belong; and some are purposely hidden away. Then there are also cases where events in mere sequence are mistaken for cause and effect. I know a case where, in the record, artillery claims to have driven away by its fire a body of infantry ; but the fact was that the infantry moved off by order, without the hostile fire having anything to do with it.

To illustrate how small may be the missing nails and yet how far-reaching and serious the result, I would point to Vinoy's successful retreat to Paris from Mezières with a small and inferior force after Sedan, in the face of a large and well-trained German force. I find that the mistakes of at least ten people of various ranks, from generals to a N.C. officer, were the missing nails that combined to the result, some of these being errors of a very minor character indeed.

Very often some of the most important details, and especially the causes of unpleasant incidents, are carefully guarded from common knowledge by the very men who know all about them. The accounts given by these men will be found in diaries or private letters to friends and relations at home. These men do not care to give others away, and, moreover, sometimes what they have written is withheld till after their death as containing, regarding men and matters, views and opinions that might injure the professional prospects of the writer.

Probably the most remarkable instance of official reticence in exposing errors in war is the line taken by the Germans with regard to the war of 1870-71.

Between 1874 and 1881 was issued the Official History of that war compiled by the German General Staff, under the supervision of von Moltke. It is in five thick volumes, and I know a good deal about their contents, as I corrected three-fourths or four-fifths of the proofs of the translation for Major Clark, the translator.

Von Moltke's production is a marvellous example of *suppressio veri* from beginning to end. Go through that book and you will seek almost in vain, in this history of the actions of human beings like ourselves, in stress and difficulty, for any record whatever of anyone in the German force having made a mistake or done anything he should not have done, and yet this book is Military History.

It seems probable that von Moltke was influenced by two considerations : first, that ere long France and Germany might find themselves again opposed to each other in the field. He would not, there-fore, admit publicly to the possible foe that any-one he had brought against them was not up to the standard and might be regarded by them as a poor commander or soldier when next encountered in the field. Second, that the German troops would in that case find over them and leading them a very large number of the same officers of various ranks who were their officers in 1870-71; and although we may be quite sure that German leaders and others occasionally went wrong and received from von Moltke full and due correction, yet he would not by public censure shake in any way the confidence in them of the men whom they might have to lead at some future time.

The result of this wholesome reticence, this suppression of facts, is, that even now we have from the German side only partial glimpses of that war.

Take that episode I have mentioned as the result of some dozen of mistakes by individuals. That episode and the failure of the German force read so naturally in the original history that they seem in no way strange. It was not until 1888, eighteen years after the event, that the German staff published the full and true account in a book of 200-300 pages, giving in the introduction as their reason that they could not allow their young officers to grow up in the erroneous belief that the operation had been properly carried out.

And this reticence is surpassed by that with which the history of the great battle of Gravelotte has been dealt with. Not until six years ago, thirty-six years after the battle, was a full account given to Germany and the world by the German General Staff.

From the Preface I will give some extracts which confirm some of the views I have put forward.

The instructional value of a record of the battle is thus given :—

" There is hardly any other battle of the Franco-Prussian War which provides such a rich store of information regarding the leading of troops —higher as well as lower—or which can so well show the conditions to be expected in a pitched battle with such great masses of troops. . . .

" Owing to the wider view which is now possible concerning men and events, there will be found certain differences between this work and that brought out by the General Staff in 1875. . . .

" We could gather in 1875 only very insufficient data regarding the conditions on the French side ; therefore upon this point great divergencies will be disclosed. . . .

" Furthermore, the knowledge of the conditions on the German side has meanwhile undergone an essential enlargement. The Royal Saxon Archives have aided the work of study.   Numerous comrades-in-arms, among them not a few highly-placed officers, have not denied their co-operation, but have most willingly disclosed their personal knowledge, and freely answered the questions put to them. It is only due to them to say that now the true lessons of that war-time—now thirty-six years behind us—can here be turned to account."

One difference deserves special notice.

Von Moltke's original plan for the battle was completely upset by the General Commanding the IXth A.C. commencing the battle prematurely. The reasons now given for this error on the part of the General are quite different from those given in the original account.

It is impossible for anyone to compare and contrast the old and the new accounts of the battle without realising that one of the chief and main characteristics of all Military History must necessarily be *Evolution*, and Evolution takes time.

And on the French side we may expect similar unexpected enlightenment. In the *Revue d'Histoire Militaire* the French General Staff is putting forward, very slowly, however, its account of the campaign of the First Army of the Loire; they have so far dealt with only about a month, the least eventful part of the campaign, but already there is in it, and specially in the number of only last December, much that promises to lead us seriously to modify some of the errors hitherto held and based on the data hitherto available.

And now let me openly admit that I regard Military History as unsatisfactory as a record of events, so soon as it deals with details, and the

I

more so as it penetrates into details ; and this
owing to the incompleteness of the evidence and
the frequent lapses from accuracy.

To sum up ; every incident in war is due, either,
it may be but very rarely, to the isolated action
of one individual, or, as is the case ordinarily, it
is the combined effect of the individual actions
of a crowd of people, some acting for success, but
others acting unintentionally for failure ; and it
is beyond possibility ever to obtain and collect
from the crowd the amount of testimony necessary
to render the record accurate and trustworthy.

It is with the General Staff of an army that
alone lies the possibility of collecting the maximum
of available data, and this will necessarily give
but a one-sided view, until the General Staff of
the army that has fought against it has published its own version of the matter.

Nevertheless my own experience affords me
much ground for consolation. After every war
there are available at once, as there were even in
1871, a very vast amount of undeniable, indisput-
able facts, fully sufficient to enable the compiler
to put together such a record as will afford a very
fair account of the war, and from the study of
which many sound lessons for future guidance
can be drawn ; and year by year the work he can
produce becomes more full and more satisfactory.
Doubtless in some cases he will be able to hit off
correctly the precise " Why ", and the precise

"How", but this will hardly be possible unless he has had before him, and has carefully compared, the cases for both sides. Otherwise, he plays the part of a counsel speaking from a brief, rather than of a judge delivering an impartial summing-up.

It is, however, the smaller incidents of a war which are so valuable as concrete illustrations of the work of the lower ranks. Of those which come to hand it may fairly be presumed that although they all have a strong basis of fact, some are leavened with a considerable amount of imagination ; still, some are absolutely true, and the others, with rare exceptions, are at all events possibilities and probabilities suited to the environment whence they came. As reliable history, however, it is well to receive them with considerable reserve. The compiler should never scorn to utilise these because he is uncertain as to the exact amount of truth they contain, but let him regard them as the branch of Military History which may be denominated " Taken on Trust " Military History.

Most valuable, most soundly educational, most necessary for the soldier is the study of Military History in spite of its weaknesses, all must admit ; only it must be utilised with care and discretion, and not in what I may call a " cock-sure " spirit ; and especially must it not be employed for advo- cating pet theories and " fads ", on evidence perhaps doubtful and one-sided.

In conclusion, let me express the hope that the more the difficulties encountered in the compilation of Military History are realised, the less severe will become the judgments of writers on military leaders ; and the less will be the inclination of a nation to pass, on incomplete and perhaps untrustworthy evidence, censure on its soldiers, when things in the field are not going well with them.

THE VALUE OF THE STUDY OF MILITARY HISTORY AS TRAINING FOR COMMAND IN WAR

BY LIEUTENANT-COLONEL F. MAURICE

FORTUNATELY it is no longer necessary to advocate the study of Military History. In our own Army as in all armies trained on modern principles this study has its established place in the military training of the officer. Indeed, I should suppose that even in England, of those who habitually study history for professional purposes, the great majority are soldiers.

I do not propose to concern myself now with the bearing of the study of history upon those larger problems of strategy which jointly concern the statesman and the soldier. Nor am I concerned with the application of the experience of recent wars either to tactical methods, or to the organisation, armament, and administration of armies. The particular aspect of this question with which I intend to deal is the use of Military History as a means of training officers for command in war.

This use of history is not always understood, even by officers, though almost all read military

history and some study it.   Many have no very
exact idea of the practical value to be obtained
or how to obtain it.   In this soldiers are not
peculiar.   In almost all professions there are
more who seek to acquire a knowledge of facts than
there are who draw deductions from that knowledge.   Yet mere knowledge of facts is of itself
of very little value, and probably of less value
to the soldier than to others.

There is a story told of the Staff College of
the days when examinations were more frequent
and more important than they are at present,
concerning a certain student who obtained a
high place by compiling a *memoria technica*,
with the help of which he was able to place accurately every company on either side at the
critical phase of the battle of Gravelotte—St Privat.
For all practical purposes the officer might, with
equal advantage, have learnt the binomial theorem
backwards.

If there is one thing more certain than another
in war it is that any one set of conditions will
never be exactly reproduced.   Therefore the mere
knowledge, say, of Napoleon's action at Austerlitz
or of Wellington's at Salamanca is of itself useless,
because the particular conditions which confronted
those great leaders on those battlefields will not
recur.

What help then can the study of history give
us in training officers for command in war ?

How can it in any way replace practical experience ?

The answer is that it cannot replace practical experience, but that it can supplement and complete experience.

Practical experience is an essential foundation, for by it alone can the soldier learn to overcome all the innumerable causes of friction and difficulty which are involved in the handling of a human machine in circumstances of stress. An officer's practical experience of command in the field is obtained at manœuvres and, if he is fortunate, in war. But from a variety of causes this experience is not of itself sufficient. Mainly for financial reasons, experience at manœuvres is only obtainable for a comparatively few days in the year; and even this experience cannot be enjoyed by all, while in the most favourable circumstances the conditions are only a faint approach to those of war.

Practical experience in war is, in normal times, exceptional. Further, we are here faced with the same phenomenon which makes mere knowledge of the facts of the past campaigns of no value—the experiences of any one campaign will never be exactly reproduced. Usually an officer who is fortunate enough to take part in a number of wars finds himself in each campaign in a different rank with different responsibilities, while in each his experience is confined to the narrow circle of his own activities. To quote from Colonel Gizyki's admirable study of the subject, " Such experience is, it is true, more comprehensive as a man rises in rank, but the superior officer misses much which only the subaltern officer experiences. The subaltern is mainly occupied with the troubles which have to be overcome in leading the rank and file, the superior officer with the friction which arises in the distribution of orders and in the conduct of the larger formations. Even within the same sphere of action, individual experiences of war may differ utterly from one another. One man has only been present at successful actions, another only at a defeat, a third may have passed through a campaign without being under fire at all. One has been in the advanced guard which has been struggling from the beginning of the day, another only reached the battlefield when the enemy's strength was broken."

History is indeed full of examples in which practical experience of war has, when undue reliance has been placed upon it, proved positively harmful. Human nature is such that habits and methods of thought which are the outcome of practical experience are not readily changed under an entirely new set of conditions.

The French entered upon the war of 1870 with a wide and varied experience of colonial warfare against ill-armed enemies under a tropical sun.

When fighting in their own country against a highly trained enemy with equal armament, they still clung to many customs which they had acquired in Northern Africa. To take one example of many, the habit of taking a narrow view and local of the functions of protective troops, which not only escaped disaster but was even justifiable when fighting native races, brought with it dire consequences when the opponent was expert, bold, and enterprising. Our own experiences in the early battles of the South African War were not dissimilar.

We require then a wider knowledge of war than is obtainable from practical experience even by the most fortunate, and to obtain this wider knowledge we must go to the records of past war. With the theoretical experience obtained by dealing with the problems which have faced the great leaders of other days, corrected by practical experience in the handling of men, a commander may hope to fit himself to deal with the innumerable permutations and combinations of war. We find the clearest and most definite support in history for this statement. For in almost every case in which we know the story of the early training of the masters of the art of war we find that they have followed some such system. So far there is little dispute; but when we come to consider exactly how history is to be used in the training of officers for command, we find some ignorance and many differences of opinion.

What are the mental qualities which are essential in a commander of troops in the field, whatever his rank may be ? They consist primarily in the capacity to form rapid and correct decisions from incomplete and conflicting data in circumstances of great difficulty. Almost every order, almost every decision which a commander is required to formulate when in the presence of the enemy, involves the solution of some such problem. In these problems only one side of the equation is known—the commander's own intention, the dispositions of his own troops. Even this is not always so, for as to the latter point, the dispositions and movements of his own troops, complete information is sometimes not to hand when it is needed. The other side of the equation, the will of the opposing commander and the dispositions and movements of his troops, can only, except in rare cases, be guessed at.

It is then necessary that the mental qualities required in the solution of such problems should be developed in commanders. In this history can help us greatly, but it is important for this purpose that it should be the right kind of history, and that the right kind of history should be treated in the right way.

Before considering what the right kind of history is and the way to make use of it, may I say that in this matter some civilian historians have done us soldiers a disservice ?   There are many histories otherwise admirable which are obliged to deal with the events of campaigns in a very short space. Partly from this reason and partly, I fear, because the writers have not grasped the various processes which go on in the mind of a commander and the nature of the problems by which he is confronted, we often find in their books a completely false conception both of the nature of war and of the qualities which make a great leader.

We are told frequently that victories by which great generals overwhelmed their opponents were inspired by flashes of genius, and that the mistakes of their opponents were due to pedantic adherence to what are called the rules of war.   We read of the thunderbolt of Austerlitz, the lightning stroke of Salamanca, and we are not given any indication that these masterpieces were the result of any previous meditation.   Yet we find him to whom above all others these flashes of genius are ascribed saying—" Je n'ai jamais rien fait par inspiration, mais beaucoup par réflexion."   And also " Ce n'est pas un génie qui me révèle tout à coup, en secret, ce que j'ai à faire ou à dire dans une circonstance inattendue par les autres, c'est la réflexion, la méditation."

The Great Duke's faculty of guessing what was happening on the other side of the hill, the apparently intuitive knowledge of what the enemy

was going to do, which is such a marked characteristic of Frederick's and of Napoleon's generalship, were in each case the outcome of severe
and concentrated thought. Each of them had
acquired the habit of thinking out, whenever
they were engaged on operations which might
bring them into contact with an enemy, both the
possible courses of action open to that enemy,
and the counter-moves required to meet each.
Thus, when the enemy decided upon some one
plan and began his movements, the orders suitable
to the circumstances were rapped out without
hesitation, since the situation had been foreseen
and provided for.

These then are distinct methods of leadership
which can be imitated and to some extent acquired
by practice. Stanhope has placed on record
of the Duke of Wellington, Carlyle has placed
on record of Frederick, and Napoleon has placed
it on record of himself, that this habit of mind,
this method, was in each case the result of continuous training and practice. But when boys—
and it is especially of the histories which are
placed in the hands of boys that I am now speaking
—when boys are told that these great feats are
the result of inspiration, they naturally deduce
that generalship is a natural and inborn quality,
and they are not the more disposed, should they
elect to become soldiers, to set much value on the
study of war.

Again, we find some historians, and amongst these are some who devote themselves more particularly to Military History, who lead us soldiers astray because they base their criticisms of generalship not on what the generals knew or should have known at the time when they formed their decisions, but on the knowledge of the complete equation which they, the writers, possess in the full light of information obtained after the event.

Such criticism is not only of no value for our purpose, but is positively harmful as giving an utterly false picture of the tasks which confront commanders in war.

The right kind of history, then, for this purpose of the training of the mind to deal with the problems involved in the leading of troops in the field, is that which gives us the fullest information as to all the factors which influenced one leader or the other in forming his decision. We want to know what the commander knew, neither more nor less; we want to be able to put ourselves in his place. We want to know what he knew or guessed about the enemy; we want to know the positions and condition of his troops, whether they were fresh, elated, and well-fed, or tired, depressed, and hungry; we want to know the conditions of the country, the state of the roads, of the weather, and the innumerable other factors which together make up a military problem.

All this can only be obtained from the official records of a war. These records are now systematically collected and digested in the history sections of the great general staffs of modern armies. But even these official histories require to be interpreted with judgment and knowledge. As regards the most important events of war, the decisive battles, they are compilations from a vast number of individual reports, written after the event, by men whose whole attention has been absorbed in the immediate task which confronted them. Times and places which the historian requires as a framework of his story are often unrecorded, or if recorded are only the result of a memory which is confused by the rush of events. Even the best history of battles is usually little more than a compromise, which is the resultant of a mass of conflicting evidence.

Further, every official historian is confronted with the difficulty that the leaders whose work he is describing are usually alive, probably many of them still in command of troops, and may again be in command in the next war. In these circumstances a frank statement of all the facts is for obvious reasons inexpedient, and these facts can only be deduced either by careful reading between the lines or by supplementing the official story from later unofficial sources.

With the help, then, of one source of information or of another we require to be able to place the student as nearly as possible in the position of the commander in the field, to give him the problem as it presented itself to that commander. Then he may be left to solve the problem for himself; or, if assistance is available, he may be shown how the problem was solved, how far the commander acted upon principles which are of universal application, or whether he was influenced by local conditions which are unlikely to recur. For the purpose of gaining experience of the problems of command, the history of all wars is not of equal value. The nearer the conditions of past wars conform to the conditions of those in which officers may be called upon to serve in the future, the more valuable will this study be to them, at least in the early stages. The great principles of strategy are commonly said to be immutable; but modern developments of means of communication have so completely changed the conditions of time and space upon which, above all other factors, strategy depends, that the history of campaigns fought before the development of railways and telegraphs is more than likely to lead the beginner astray, if he is set to study them by the light of nature ; and it is at least doubtful whether the labour necessary to dress the old conditions in a form applicable to contemporary war might not more profitably be expended in other ways.

I am aware that Napoleon has told us to read

and re-read the campaigns of Alexander, Hannibal, Caesar, Gustavus, Turenne, Eugène and Frederick ; that is, for the time when this advice was given, the history of recent and of ancient war. I may say by the way that this maxim of the great Emperor has, like many others, been grievously misinterpreted ; and this misinterpretation has induced many to believe that there is some definite advantage to be gained from much reading, whereas he certainly meant to imply, and showed by example, that the gain lies in much thinking. Until Napoleon's master mind doubled and trebled the mobility of armies by his system of supplying and marching his troops, the fundamental factors of strategy had not altered materially. Claudius Nero's marches from Venusia to the Metaurus to defeat Hasdrubal and back south to confront Hannibal are as fine an example of operations on interior lines, of the value of mobility, and of just appreciation of the factors of time and space, as anything to be found in the campaigns of Turenne and Frederick. For Napoleon's purpose the value of the study of such operations had not become stale by time. But if we can conceive Hannibal and Hasdrubal as being connected by wireless telegraphy, the very basis of the problem which Nero solved with such success is changed.

It may be gathered from what I have said that I include Napoleon's campaigns in the category of those which are of practical value at the present day, though they belong to a pre-railway and pre-telegraph era. This is, I think, incontestable. Many quite recent developments of war—for example, the present system of marching armies, and to some extent the methods of employing cavalry —have been rediscovered by modern students of Napoleonic war. I am, however, strongly of opinion that a beginning should be made with the most recent wars of which we have complete or reasonably complete information, and that a study of later campaigns should be deferred until the student has thoroughly grasped the problems involved in the leading of troops under existing conditions. The special value of these campaigns lies in the fact that the great Frenchman revolutionised war, as it was known in the eighteenth century, as completely as modern invention has done in the twentieth.

I do not mean to imply that it is only the work and thought of the great commanders of great armies which are of value to us. Military History provides us with numberless examples of situations which have been met successfully and unsuccessfully by commanders in every rank of bodies of troops of all sizes. This greatly enlarges the scope of the experience which can be gained from history. The essential in every case is that the problem should be in a real sense a military problem.

K

I am not presumptuous enough to suppose that I have here put forward anything original or new. But I do believe that the question of obtaining practical value from the study of Military History is not always fully understood either by English soldiers or by English military historians. The aspect of this question which I have put before you has for a long time been kept in view at the Staff College, and both my father and Henderson habitually used the methods I have endeavoured to describe.

Lord Wolseley speaking twenty years ago said:—

" As far as my knowledge of the study of the art of war goes the great thing is to read little and to think a great deal—to think it over and over again."

My father wrote in 1887 :—

" In all professional study it is essential for a soldier at all events to keep before him that the object is not to acquire information concerning operations, but to improve his judgement as to what ought to be done under the varied conditions of actual war."

" By far the most useful way of studying Military History," said Henderson a few years later, " is to find out what the situation was at any given time, then to shut the books, take the map and decide for yourself what you would have done had you been in the place of one of the commanding generals."

These three quotations summarise what I have tried to put before you as to the methods of using as a means of training for command. By re-creating the problems which have confronted the leaders of the past, and by comparing our own solutions with theirs, we train our intelligence, in the words of Napoleon, " to reject methods contrary to those adopted by those great men."

THE PRACTICAL APPLICATION OF MILITARY HISTORY

BY LIEUTENANT-COLONEL N. MALCOLM

I HOPE that this meeting will not consider that I am claiming too much when I say that Military History should be the most constructive branch of what is essentially a constructive science. If he is to do any real good the teacher of Military History must have his thoughts permanently fixed upon the future. In that way only can he turn such knowledge as he possesses to a useful end.

If this is true of Military History as a whole, it is more particularly true of that part of it which deals with tactics—the part upon which I propose to touch to-day. Strategy has a few permanent principles, of which the most important is that it should enable a commander to bring more men on to the field of battle than his opponent. Tactics, I think, have only one principle, and that is that men should be so handled that they can use whatever weapons they possess to the best advantage. Assuming that soldiers of all armies are equally well trained, and animated by equally high courage, the art of the general will consist in so handling his men that they can use their weapons to greater effect than can their opponents. The question is, how can this art be learnt? The answer is, from experience or from history. In practice it is usually learnt from history corrected by more or less bitter experience.

From this it seems to follow that in teaching (either oneself or others) tactics by far the most useful history is the most recent. But that is not, I think, altogether true. It requires a great deal of qualification. The one thing which the commander of to-day wishes to know is what a battle will be like if he is called upon to fight to-morrow. It seems clear, therefore, that the best thing he can do is to get in his mind a picture of the battle which was fought yesterday. A visit to Lule Burgas or to Liao-Yang will be of more use to him than a detailed knowledge of all the fighting which took place up to the end of the South African War.

If, however, instead of being fought to-morrow the battle does not take place for ten years, the case is entirely altered. It is then that history comes in, for it is only by knowing how things have come to be what they are that he can form any idea as to what they are likely to become in the future.

We have the highest authority for saying that tactics change every ten years; and history shows us that those changes have followed a regular course of development and have been almost invariably brought about by improved weapons, by improvements in the means of killing. To this rule there appears to be one exception, and that is that from time to time armies may appear to be animated with a spirit of fanaticism which defies all rules. Of this exception the French revolutionary wars provide, I suppose, the most striking example. Then, as Mr Herbert Fisher has said, "Armies for the first time came to be regarded not as royal capital to be saved, but as national income to be expended." And so in these wars we see for a time a distinct change in battles, brought about not by improved weapons but by a peculiar spirit. Such a change must be always a reversion to a more primitive but extraordinarily effective type.

Time showed the weak point in this new aspect of war; and it was then seen that this form of income, like other forms, had its limits. The means of killing gained the upper hand, and tactics resumed their normal course of development.

I do not mean to trace that course. But let me be quite clear on one point; that is, that I do not mean to convey the impression that battles will go to the army which possesses the best weapons. If it were not for the teaching of history we might easily fall into that error ; but history teaches us that success has gone to the nations which have known how to adapt their tactics so as to meet the improvements in their opponents' weapons. The rapid development of tactics in the Japanese armies after the battle of Nan Shan is a good illustration of my point.

Looking back from where we are at present we can see that improvements in weapons have brought about three results :—

(1) Greatly increased battle-fronts.

(2) Enhanced value of cover.

(3) Longer battles.

As an instance of these developments we may take the two battles of Königgrätz and the Sha Ho —1866 and 1904. On both occasions the numbers engaged were something like 400,000 men. Yet in 1866 the battle was fought over a front of eight miles and was over in a day ; in 1904 the front was forty miles and the battle lasted more than a week.

A fourth result, less generally recognised, is great rapidity of movement in the field accompanied by long hours during which no movement is possible. Something of the kind seems to have happened in Thrace, but we have not yet sufficient data to draw any useful deductions.

This is where Military History helps us. We see how these changes have been brought about, and it seems fair to assume that similar improvements in weapons will in the future produce similar effects upon tactics; and the student of war will, if he is wise, always watch present-day developments of the means of killing, while history will help him to see what effect those developments are likely to have upon tactics.

As an instance of what I mean I would quote two papers written by von Moltke for the information of the King of Prussia, in 1858 and 1868 respectively. In those papers he examines very carefully the recent improvements in arms and the effect that they are likely to have. To help him to form his opinion he carefully examines Napoleon's campaigns; it is by the light of those campaigns that he forms his conclusions; and upon those conclusions the Prussian armies were trained. That is the true use of Military History—its practical application to existing conditions. Doubtless von Moltke was not always right. His forecasts were not always correct. It is also true that we shall not always have a von Moltke to do our prophesying; but if we follow his example we shall be on the right lines, and if we use our history as he used his we shall make fewer mistakes than we should do otherwise.

In conclusion let me give an example of my theory. Since the Russo-Japanese War there has been no very striking change in infantry weapons. That being so, history leads us to believe that no material change in tactics will be brought about by rifle-fire. If rifles only were to be considered, the opening battles of the next great war would be very like the Sha Ho and Mukden, due allowance being made for topographical differences.

In other directions there have, however, been great and far-reaching changes—notably air-craft and quick-firing artillery. Air-craft we may put on one side, as although they will produce great changes they will hardly affect minor tactics. They will affect the Commander-in-Chief; but they will not affect the man in the ranks, with whom we are at present concerned.

That is not the case with artillery. Not only have we got the remarkable development of quick-firing artillery which had its origin in France, but every army now takes into the field various forms of heavy artillery. In Germany two kinds of howitzer—heavy and light—form part of every army corps.

What the effect of all this artillery is going to be no one can say. It is going to cause great surprises in the opening battles of the next great war, and every General Staff must make some forecast and amend its training accordingly. Again I say their only guide is history; and even though they may be unconscious of the fact, history *will* be their guide.

So far as I can see, the tendency of artillery improvements has been not exactly extra ex-

tension of the line either of attack or defence,
but definite breaks in that line, so that during daylight, at all events, considerable stretches of country
will be protected by fire alone.   In place of the
old continuous line of battle to which we are more
or less accustomed, we may expect to see a series
of isolated actions, the intervening ground being
rendered impassable merely by the rapidity and
range of modern artillery fire.   The valley of the
Ta-ssu at the battle of Liao-Yang brook is a case
in point.

Further speculation upon the characteristics
of the next great battle forms a fascinating sport.
Certainly there will be a great increase in night-
fighting, and it is not impossible that those armies
which have not already done so may find it necessary to add search-light apparatus to their already
cumbersome impedimenta.

This matter of night operations forms an
excellent illustration of the importance of the
most recent experience.   Until even the end of
the South African War a night march was a
common prelude to an attack at dawn.   That is
to say, the hours of darkness were used to effect
surprise.   Night operations were the *first* phase
of the battle.   The Russo-Japanese War started
a new era.   Then for the first time we see darkness
used absolutely for cover, to enable troops to
cross a fire-swept zone which had been impassable
by daylight ; and so the night assault became not

the initial but the crowning act. That new experience seems to have been repeated in Thrace ; and we may, I think, reasonably expect it to be confirmed in the next war.

And so I return to the point from which I began, which is to lay stress upon the constructive side of our branch of history ; and to say that although we may read and re-read the campaigns of great commanders, it must be principally with a view to forming a picture of what the next great war is going to be like.

PRÉCIS OF THE PLANS OF NAPOLEON FOR THE AUTUMN CAMPAIGN OF 1813

BY DR J. HOLLAND ROSE

THE sweeping condemnation passed by Jomini on Napoleon's conduct in granting to the Allies the armistice of 4th June–10th August, 1813, is open to question ; for the Emperor's positions near Breslau were menaced by Austria, whose partiality for the Allies was already observable. Further, he needed not only to reform his cavalry but also to construct an intrenched camp which would secure his communications with France. This had to be at Dresden, which was at that time weakly defended. He also wished to assure his hold on Hamburg. His neglect to appease Austria during the armistice resulted from resentment, from contempt of her resources, and from confidence in the defensive capacity of the line of the Elbe. He decided against withdrawal to the River Saal. Dangers of the Elbe line and measures taken for the strengthening of Dresden. A blow by the Allies at his communications would be met by a dash from the Zittau pass against Prague. As usual, Napoleon underestimated the enemies' strength.

The weakness of Dresden at the beginning of the autumn campaign led him on 12th August to plan a strict defensive within easy reach of that city, but on 13th August he developed his plans so as to include a pursuit of Blücher's Silesian army and an eventual move into Bohemia. Meanwhile Oudinot was to drive Bernadotte's northern army from Berlin, Davout assisting from Hamburg by a blow at its communications. Consideration of Napoleon's plans for Hamburg and the operations in that quarter (Hamburg to become in 1814 a great dockyard for extensive naval operations against England). Consequent diffusion of his strength from the essential points, those at and near Dresden. Warnings of Marmont as to the need of concentration. The Emperor's scheme broke down on the circumference of his operations ; but his timely concentration at Dresden led to the last of his great victories.

The term " a limited offensive " is inexact as applied to Napoleon's operations against Berlin, which aimed ultimately at the relief of French garrisons at Küstrin, Stettin, and, if possible, at Dantzig. The disaster to Macdonald at the Katzbach also enabled Blücher finally to join Bernadotte ; and the failure of the concentric moves on Berlin involved the isolation of Davout at Hamburg. The radical defects of the Emperor's plans were the excessive length of the Elbe-line—Königstein to Hamburg—and the advance at too many points and at too great distances from that base, which led to the independent action of subordinates unequal to the duties imposed on them. Finally, the concentration on Leipzig of the allied Grand Army and those of Blücher and Bernadotte necessitated the abandonment of the Elbe line along with five French garrisons along its course.

The issue of the campaign does not necessarily prove the impossibility of holding an extended river line against superior forces ; for that plan (the original plan) was extended and complicated by the addition of others which proved impossible of execution. The concentration of the Allies on Napoleon's line of communication falsified his declaration on 17th August to St Cyr—" Peu m'importe qu'on nous coupe de France."

Note.—The full text of Dr Rose's article appears in the *Edinburgh Review* for October 1913.

THE INFLUENCE OF TACTICAL IDEAS ON WARFARE

BY L. S. AMERY

IT is, I know, a rash proceeding to appraise the importance of any single factor in the complicated and shifting field of military history. And if I venture on this occasion to rush in where more competent historians would fear to tread, and hazard a few generalisations on the influence of certain tactical ideas, I do it, not in the expectation of making any contribution to your knowledge, but in the hope that, possibly, my rough and imperfectly based conclusions may suggest a useful line of inquiry. I ought, perhaps, to begin by making it clear that in using the expression " tactical idea " I am not referring so much to the idea of the commander in disposing his forces for action, as to something much more elementary, namely, the general idea or style of fighting in which the ordinary soldier is trained— the ultimate factor which underlies leadership in the field and in the campaign. Military history, like most other history, is usually surveyed from the top downwards. We study the political and economic motives and causes of a war, we follow the operations of strategy, we pore over the dispositions of the battlefield, and then, lastly, we note the fighting equipment and methods of the ordinary soldier. But it may not be amiss, for once in a way, to invert the order of importance, treat the soldier and his notion of fighting as the dominating element, and relegate the great generals and the fate of empires and civilisations to a secondary and consequential position. And why not ? Without the idea of infantry shock tactics, without the heavily armed and highly drilled hoplite, there could have been no Marathon and no Arbela, no Miltiades and no Alexander, no Sophocles and no Euclid. Without open order and the *pilum* there would have been no Scipio and no Trajan, consequently no Roman Empire and no modern Europe.

It is, of course, true that every tactical system has, in its turn, depended on its social, economic and political environment. Both the hoplite and the legionary postulated, not only a considerable level of material wellbeing and artificership for their equipment, but also the stable political organisation required for the prolonged collective training which alone could secure their efficiency. Modern engineering, modern commerce and modern luxury have, between them, created the petrol-engine, the motor-car, and finally the aëroplane, with consequences that may be revolutionary for the whole art of war. Similarly, every tactical system has, at some time or other, owed much to the insight of some general or statesman, a Philip of Macedon, an Edward I. or a Frederick William, who in the method of fighting he found to hand has grasped an underlying tactical idea and developed it with boldness and logical consistency. Nevertheless it is worth while to take the various leading tactical ideas or systems in isolation, to see if we can find any principle of success common to them which may cast a light both on their history and on the problems of modern warfare.

The essence of the Greek military system lay in its absolute concentration of purpose on a single tactical idea, that of shock. In Homeric times the spear was used for hurling as well as for charging, and made to suit either emergency, in consonance with the individualist character of primitive war. The early tacticians of classical Greece resolutely suppressed the temptation to use the spear for any purpose but the charge, and made everything subserve the one object of giving that charge the maximum effect. The long spear, the heavy protective armour, and above all the absolute precision of drill, gave the solid wall of hoplites a cohesion and a momentum against which no less well-trained force could stand. More than two thousand years later the savage Dingiswayo, watching British soldiers at their drill, carried the same notion of shock tactics home to his kraal : within a generation the Zulu *impis* had devastated all the interior of South Africa, laid open the country to the Boer *voortrekkers*, and so shaped the whole course of South African history.

For a century and a half Greek shock tactics remained substantially unchanged. It was a semi-barbarian ruler, Philip of Macedon, who conceived the idea of pressing the idea of shock tactics to its logical conclusion, by enormously lengthening the spears of the rear ranks, thus multiplying the spear-heads available at the point of impact, and locking the ranks together in a solid wooden framework. Philip made the phalanx ; it remained for Alexander to conquer half the known world with its help. The phalanx represented infantry shock tactics *in excelsis*. There never has been any formation of troops unprovided with long range weapons, whether mounted or on foot, which could stand up against the phalanx on level ground.

Meanwhile the Romans, out of touch with the main current of Greek military tradition, were developing an entirely different system of their own. Beginning apparently with a front line of spear throwers preceding the charge of the main body, they gradually eliminated the charge altogether, and modified both armament and tactics to secure the utmost efficiency from the use of the spear as a short-range projectile. The spear itself was shortened and deliberately rendered useless for charging. For troops who had no intention of charging home, close order was obviously superfluous. The Romans not only broke up the solid front of battle into a scheme of detached maniples arranged in *quincunx* or harrow formation, but drew up their men individually in a similar open order, which enabled rank after rank successively to run forward and hurl its *pila*. Such a formation not only provided the heaviest possible fire of projectiles, but opposed to the enemy's charge a yielding, elastic framework against which its momentum would be spent in vain. Further, the fact that the Roman formation covered a larger front and was as effective on broken ground or on a hillside as on the level plain, added immensely to its value as an all-round instrument of war.

Such a system for its full effectiveness demanded a perfection of discipline and a moral steadiness even greater than that required for the phalanx. In the early stages of its development it could hardly have made headway against well-drilled Greek troops; and if Rome and Greece had come into contact in the fifth century the Roman system would probably have perished in its immaturity. As it was, each of the two systems had practically reached its full development when they met. The legion never fairly beat the phalanx on the level. But it won the day on its all-round merits, and for five centuries it held the field. It passed away, not because a superior system rose in its place, but because the underlying conditions of its success had disappeared. It had grown to greatness as the expression of the strength and resolve of an armed and free community. As the professional police of an Empire as unmilitary almost as that of China, it was forced to modify its methods, and lost its essential spirit. It was not the legion as such, but the inherent weakness of the Roman political system, that collapsed before the onset of the Gothic horsemen at Adrianople.

The succeeding centuries show, outside of the Eastern Empire, not a progress, but a decline in the art of war. The mediæval army was simply the embodiment of the political disorganisation of the day. The knights in armour represented the most effective system for fighting on a small scale in the absence of any organisation for collective training. Their occasional collection in considerable numbers did not make them really formidable as an army. The mob of ill-armed and wholly untrained footmen which accompanied them exemplified even more visibly the lack of real energy in the loosely coherent and unorganised national community. When a new and really formidable tactical system arose in Western Europe, it arose not unnaturally in the one country which enjoyed a stronger monarchy and a more effective national organisation than the rest. Edward I., who had learnt to realise the possibilities of the long-bow in his Welsh campaigns, had the power as well as the insight to make of the English a nation of archers. The wars with the Scots enabled the new system to overcome the experimental stage and to acquire a definite method of working both as regards the archers themselves and as regards the backing of dismounted men-at-arms. For nearly a century after Creçy the English archers remained invincible. The secret of their success lay in the thoroughness with which the nation was trained to the use of the bow; in the boldness with which English generalship discarded tradition and trusted whole-heartedly to the new method of warfare, subordinating to it everything else, even the ordinary use of the knights in armour, on which the rest of Europe relied; and not least in that imperturbable steadiness which at all times has been the greatest fighting asset of the English soldier.

The English archer was not the only adversary before whom the feudal military system had to give way in the fourteenth and fifteenth centuries. Courtrai, Morgarten, Sempach and Morat showed that, with the growth of independent communities of freemen, the old idea of infantry shock tactics could once again assert its efficacy. But at this point the normal course of military evolution was interrupted by the discovery of firearms. The interruption, however, was only partial. For while the killing power of the new weapon exceeded anything previously known, it was by no means sufficiently formidable in respect either of range, accuracy, or rapidity of fire to make it possible for the older weapons to be wholly dispensed with.   The development of infantry shock tactics continued with Swiss and German and Spanish pikemen, in steadily closer combination with the use of firearms.   As the latter improved the pikemen were reduced in numbers, till the invention of the bayonet caused the two tactical processes to be blended in one.   This blend, or compromise, between firing tactics and shock tactics has underlain the whole tactical development of modern European warfare.

During this period of tactical compromise two main systems or schools of thought have at intervals contended for mastery.   The first was the linear system.   The object of that system was to secure the greatest possible volume of fire as a preliminary to the charge.   Steadiness and precision were the two things most essential to this system, and no one aimed at the discipline requisite to insure these qualities more wholeheartedly than Frederick William I. of Prussia. The result was the magnificent instrument of war with which Frederick the Great achieved his victories.   The line was a method only serviceable with highly trained troops, and one which appealed more particularly to the steady Teutonic temperament. The French spirit never wholly acquiesced in it, and in the wars of the Revolution new conditions arose which made the attainment of efficiency in linear tactics impossible. Von Binder-Krieglstein, in his admirable work *Geist und Stoff im Kriege*, shows in close detail how the impetuous, ill-trained French levies, face to face with the highly disciplined lines of Prussians or Austrians, gradually turned their own tactical weaknesses to account, while taking the fullest advantage of the great numerical superiority with which the immense national energy of the Revolution supplied them. Unable to stand up to their opponents in the open, they discovered that there was no reason, after all, why they should not fight on broken ground, and where cover was procurable ; without the discipline to maintain a steady line under fire, they found the column a more suitable formation for French impetuousness, preparing the way for its attack by a cloud of skirmishers. What began as the shifts of unskilled enthusiasts became a formidable system of tactics which. under Napoleon, made France, for a time, mistress of Europe. Other armies modified their methods to meet the French onset, but without abandoning their linear principle. The improvement of firearms in the last century has modified tactics still further.

But the two schools of thought still remain. The Germans hold fast throughout to the idea of the line, as giving the greatest fire-effect ; the French hold to the idea of the column, and the attack concentrated on one point. German strategy, corresponding, as strategy always should, with the tactics on which it is based, adheres to the advance of all forces in line, and to enveloping attacks. French strategy keeps large masses in reserve to throw in at the critical point, when the preliminary contact has determined that point. British tactics and strategy, which in the Napoleonic wars beat the French columns off the field by applying the principle of the line more whole-heartedly than ever, have since then, I fear, stagnated into text-book theories of war which try to embody the best of both systems and inevitably fail to secure the real advantages of either.

I have spoken of the whole period from the fifteenth century onwards as one of tactical compromise, because two wholly different ideas, the idea of fire-effect and the idea of the charge, have always underlain its fighting methods. And that is still true of the European armies of the present day. However great the improvement in the range, accuracy and rapidity of the modern firearm, however few the instances in our time of any actual effective use of bayonet or lance in action, the idea of the charge as the actual aim of the battle still dominates the training of troops and the whole planning of battles. The close order suitable to the charge is still treated as the normal formation. It is with this that the recruit begins. It is from this that the line is opened out for the actual advance under fire. It is to this that the advance is supposed to re-converge, after the prelude and preparation of the fire fight, for the final effort of the charge home. This tradition-bound system is not confined to the European nations among whom it originated. It has been handed on, as the last word of military science, to Servians and Bulgarians, Turks and Japanese, who have made good or bad use of it in accordance with their general national efficiency.

There is only one example of a military system based on pure fire-tactics. In a remote corner of the world the Boers, in the course of the nineteenth century, developed a system of warfare which looked to the firearm alone and was absolutely uncontaminated by tradition or reminiscence of any other weapon. The Boer went out to shoot his enemy as he went out to shoot game. He no more wanted to charge Zulus or British than he wanted to charge lions or elephants ; his one object in either case was to reach a position whence he could get a fair shot without undue risk. His ordinary means of locomotion, his pony, enabled him to get to such a position quickly.

The more extended the chain of these positions, the greater the opportunities for cross-fire and eventual envelopment. Loose extensions were the natural corollary of the system, and fitted in with the independent, self-reliant character of the Boers. There was no recognised normal formation, no definite distance between individuals either laterally or vertically—these things were left to be regulated by the ground itself. The same loose extensions which served so well for the concentration of aimed fire, presented practically no target to unaimed volley-firing, and offered no solid object upon which a charge could take effect. Again and again in the early stages of the war British troops deployed the whole elaborate preparation of the conventional European battle for a final blow, which, if it ever did come off proved to be a mere blow in the air. Truly typical of the singleness of view of the Boer was the complete contempt he showed, from first to last, for the use of any weapon but the rifle. In the course of the last war the Boers repeatedly charged home with the utmost gallantry, on horse or on foot, by night or day, when the occasion demanded it, but never with any other idea than that of shooting at close quarters. By the end of the war the commandos were almost completely rearmed with captured British rifles. I have never heard of a Boer even troubling to pick up a sword or a bayonet. It no more occurred to him to carry about pieces of sharpened metal than it did to fill his pockets with a few big stones which might also conceivably serve as weapons in an emergency.

The whole Boer system, in fact, however imperfectly organised, was ruthlessly logical and consistently concentrated on one object, the most efficient way to shoot men. How efficient that method was may be inferred from the fact that Boer farmers, untrained and undisciplined, but possessed of a very definite notion of how to fight, almost invariably proved a match for two or three times their number of trained British troops. It is no use trying to explain this away by dwelling on the difficulties of the ground ; there never was ground more suitable to ordinary infantry or cavalry tactics. Nor can the South African War be simply dismissed as anomalous ; it was only so in the sense that all wars are anomalous. Least of all can it be used as a plea for the amateur and undisciplined soldier. The true answer, I would venture to suggest, is that the Boers attained so remarkable a measure of success, in spite of every defeat due to want of organisation and discipline, simply because their logical and self-consistent tactics were so infinitely superior to the inconsistent and confused blend of rifle and pike tactics which we shared with the rest of Europe. No ghost of a pikeman trailed behind the Boer to cloud his impulses and confuse his judgment. Whether as leader or as follower he attained to efficiency because the object in his mind was a single and clear one.

And that conclusion I venture to think is borne out by the examples I have given earlier. Throughout history success has gone with those who have taken a tactical principle and worked it out fearlessly to its logical conclusion, suppressing all temptation to compromise with the weapons or methods of a different principle. And success has been most striking where, as in the case of the Macedonians, the Romans, the English archers, or the Boers, the new tactical system has been developed apart, and has differed most widely from the systems it has had to meet. It is possible to dream of a new English system of tactics based on a bold adaptation and improvement of the Boer system, just as the first great English system of tactics, which surprised the Middle Ages, was based on Edward I.'s adaptation of the use of the long-bow from the Welsh. How such a system could be worked out, how it could be made to fit in with the use of artillery on a large scale, how it would lend itself to combination with aëroplane work, and minimise the risks of reconnaissance by hostile aircraft, suggests a fascinating theme on which I will not venture to embark. The only conclusion I will venture to submit is that in the future, as in the past, war will be revolutionised and the face of the world altered by some power which will have the courage to break away from tradition, and to develop an entirely new system of tactics suited to the national character, and making the utmost use of every development of science available for fighting purposes.

FIELD-MARSHAL
PRINCE SCHWARZENBERG

A CHARACTER SKETCH

BY DR J. F. NOVÁK

THIS year it is a hundred years since the fate of Europe was decided at the battle of Leipzig. Upon scarcely any of the commanders who were sent out by Europe, united to fight for liberty against Napoleon, have such various judgments been pronounced, as upon the Commander-in-Chief of the allied armies himself, Marshal Prince Schwarzenberg; with the exception of some isolated voices, he has till recently remained unappreciated. His letters to his wife in the years 1799-1813, which were hitherto quite unknown and which the centenary of the battle of Leipzig has enabled me to publish, give us the first deep glimpse into his innermost being. These letters are written from heart to heart and, by reason of their intimacies and ingenuousness, are a historical source of unique value. On the basis which they provide, it is possible to form a picture of Marshal Schwarzenberg in more living colours than was till now possible. I shall proceed, of course with the greatest brevity, to give some of the most necessary biographical dates.

Prince Charles Schwarzenberg was descended from the Bohemian aristocracy. He was born in 1771 at Vienna, but his favourite seat was his castle in Bohemia, Orlík (Worlik) on the Vltava (Moldau), and he always felt strongly that he belonged to the Bohemians.[1]

Destined from his youth for a military career, he took part in the Turkish war of 1788-1789, and afterwards in all the wars that the Austrian Empire waged against France till the fall of Napoleon. During this time he was employed in diplomatic missions: in the years 1801 and 1809 he was sent to St Petersburg, and then in 1809-1812 to the Court of Napoleon at Paris. When in 1812 Austria was obliged to supply Napoleon with an auxiliary force of 30,000 men, for his campaign against Russia, Schwarzenberg was put at its head. In this campaign he was appointed Field-

[1] He tells us this in the draft of his reply to the ovations offered him by the "Estates" of Bohemia, after the victory at Leipzig. This draft has been preserved in the Archives at Orlík (see *Briefe*, p. 35):—"I have always been proud," he says, "to belong to the valiant Bohemians, but this feeling had never grown more animated and vivid in me, than in that never-to-be-forgotten moment when nothing could shake the courage of this noble people. The great events through which we have lived would never have been accomplished, if Bohemia had not co-operated for the great and sacred purpose, with unexampled persistence and endurance, shunning no sacrifice. Honoured fellow-countrymen, accept the expression of my warmest feelings of thanks, and be assured that, next to the satisfaction shown by the beloved monarch, nothing could be more flattering for me than the approval of my fellow-citizens."

Marshal at the instigation of Napoleon himself.
In the War of Liberation he was placed at the
head of the armies of the European Coalition
against Napoleon, whom he defeated in the battle
of Leipzig on the 16th-19th of October and whom
he pursued into France.   At the end of his military
career he became President of the Imperial
Military Council; but, embittered by the intrigues
set on foot against him, he became ill in 1817 and
soon afterwards died in Leipzig, 1820.   His body
was conveyed to Bohemia.   In the year 1799 he
had married the beautiful Countess Mary Annie
Hohenfeld, the widowed Princess Esterhazy, to
whom he clung with deep affection till his death.
In his letters he laid bare all his complaints and his
longings, in them his character is reflected as in a
mirror.

One of the principal traits in the character of
Marshal Schwarzenberg is his deep love for
humanity.   His humanity is not only a veneer
borrowed from the French culture of the
eighteenth century, but it is an organic part
of his whole being, and directs all the actions
of his life.   Perhaps we may find its origin in
his education, but, more likely still, in his innate
kindliness and in his study of the French
philosophers of the eighteenth century, whose
works had a prominent place in his library.   The
beautiful copies of their works in handsome
bindings with the Marshal's " ex libris ", which

are to be found in the Prince's library at Orlík, in Bohemia, bear witness to his delight in this literature. In the letters of Prince Schwarzenberg to his wife, we also find proofs of his high regard for humanity. In the letter of January 20th, 1806, the Prince reproaches Napoleon for the devastations made by his orders in the land before his departure, when he was at the culminating point of his power after the battle of Slavkov (Austerlitz), and he says :—" The weaklings with whom the world is swarming are worthless, and the greatest men, the meteors, are of no value for humanity." When writing to his wife on February 14th, 1810, after the conclusion of the marriage-contract between Napoleon and Mary Louise, Prince Schwarzenberg, then Austrian ambassador at Paris, also mentioned what a stir the report of this transaction would cause at Vienna. He says: "All I can tell you, my Annie, is my deep conviction, that I was serving my country and humanity well." He meant that, by bringing about this contract, he removed from his country the danger of war, which would have resulted if Napoleon's request had been refused.

War and humanity are two incompatible conceptions. Marshal Schwarzenberg himself felt this incompatibility, and although his fate destined him to a military career, he did not find happiness and satisfaction in this profession. He says in a letter of March 22nd, 1799, which he writes to his wife

M

while on outpost duty before the battle of Stockach, that his heart will never be accustomed to this profession, but that very often he must own with sorrow that his mind seems to impose on him the melancholy duty of making use of the military talent which he thinks he possesses. Only as quite a young officer did he look upon war with different eyes, as he admits later during the Russian campaign of 1812. In his letter of September 18th, from Holuby, he tells his wife about the skirmishes between the cossacks and the hussars, and says that those combats are a festival for a man who is young and full of fight, but he adds :—" I am sorry, I have not that feeling any more." We find a similar sigh in the letter of August 9th, 1812 :—" Oh, may I only find again that enthusiasm for the profession of arms, which I had in my young manhood."

In the terrible retreat after the battle of Hohenlinden he describes his impressions in the letter of December 16th, 1800, from Frankenmarkt :—" I can scarcely bear to look upon the evil which is entailed in the prolongation of the war and which is always before my eyes like a horrible picture ; and yet there is in it all a certain fascination, which will not allow one to leave it." When after the battle of Hohenlinden he enumerates his casualties, his heart turns away from the laurels of war with these words :—" Oh, my Annie, how sad is a profession, whose laurels are derived from the innumerable afflictions of so many people." [1]

Perhaps the greatest aversion from war was created in Marshal Schwarzenberg by the horrible devastations of the Russian campaign of 1812. In one letter of this war, written from Kivatice on November 23rd, 1812, we read : " Suffering from wind and frost I arrived here this evening, where there were spread before my eyes all the horrors of warfare at this season and in these countries. On all sides one sees nothing but frost, snow, ice, and winter, which vents its full force on the poor suffering men. In a little, miserable, wind-swept room I mourned over the state of affairs, deeply moved in my heart of hearts by the cruel fate of so many thousands." At another time in the Russian war he could not bear to see the plunderings of the Saxons, who were for a time under his command, but he could not make use of radical disciplinary measures, not knowing how long they would be entrusted to his command. On this occasion he spoke as follows about war in general : " War is a shameful thing. What terrible pictures are to be seen daily—lamentation, misery, vices of all sorts, mocking misfortunes, brutal atrocity. In a word, the heart of a just man is stirred ten times a day ; and nothing can eradicate these feelings." [2]

[1] The Prince Schwarzenberg's letter to his wife from Mühldorf, December 7th, 1800.

[2] The Marshal's letter to his wife from Rudnia, of August 19th, 1812.

In the letter of December 28th, 1812, from Ostrow in Russian Poland, he unburdens his heart with these words : "I repeat, I shall never be happy in this profession. Even if my undertaking is successful I am filled with horror. My way to happiness will never be through blood and corpses. If there is a heaven and a hell, woe to the man, who being quite conscious of his acts ventures to open this veritable Pandora's box for his fellow-creatures." These words from the mouth of a general who had taken part in many wars, and who had fought in many battles, are of greater weight than a thousand utterances of the most ardent apostles of peace.

In December 1812, already anticipating the fate of Napoleon's army in Russia, Schwarzenberg spoke as follows :—" The French army will probably be in a hazardous condition, without any cavalry at this season, tired and dissatisfied. This picture is not a bright one—death in all forms. I would not like to have on my conscience the suffering of so many millions." [1] Marshal Schwarzenberg justified defensive war only as being righteous, while war in general he termed a repulsive business, " ein empörendes Geschäft." [2] He says that he feels disgusted with war on account of the innumerable afflictions which war

---

[1] The Marshal's letter to his wife from Slonim of December 11th, 1812.

[2] The Marshal's letter to his wife from Nesviž of July 28th, 1812.

spreads over the land in all conceivable forms.[1] This general's opinion on war is very surprising, and may be described as the negative result of his humanity. Its positive result is seen in the treatment of his army. His declaration that a commander is responsible for every life sacrificed is very well known, because with every lost life are torn tender ties, and every lost life causes shedding of tears. These principles guided all his operations in war. He hated nothing more than useless shedding of blood. When in 1814 Napoleon was pursued into France, the Russians and Prussians insisted on the allied armies getting at any price as far as Paris, although it would have been possible to make an advantageous peace beforehand without any further fighting. Marshal Schwarzenberg complains in the letter of February 20th, 1814, from Troyes, that rivers of blood must now be shed to make the peace, which some days previously had been offered to the Allies, the only fault of which in the eyes of the unscrupulous was that it had not been signed in Paris. " You would not believe, my own Annie," he adds, " how indignant I feel in the depths of my heart. My situation is really a painful one."

Czar Alexander's longing to reach Paris at any price, and the vehement advance of Blücher, are characterised by Marshal Schwarzenberg in the

[1] The Marshal's letter to his wife from Ostrow of December 28th, 1812.

letter from Troyes of February 11th, 1814, as follows :—" Czar Alexander . . . persists in marching on to Paris, and I am afraid we shall pay for this by rivers of blood ; and the battles are always great crises and their results are often unexpected. My old Blücher is drawn with such a force to the Palais Royal, that again he begins to rush forward without any sense, forgetting that the enemy before him is weak, it is true, but that nevertheless an army is standing at his flank." Three days after, he says that he continues the fighting only with the greatest reluctance and is going into a battle, which, if it were successful, would only heighten the vanity of the Allies, and, if it were unsuccessful, would result in endless confusion.

When criticising the battles and operations of Marshal Schwarzenberg we must not forget his generous traits of character. He preferred cautious manœuvring, and very often defeated the enemy by well-arranged operations rather than by sharp attacks with great shedding of blood. Of course, when necessary, he was capable of the latter too. It is characteristic of the hero of cavalry attacks, who astonished the world by his personal gallantry, and who staked his life again and again, that he was embarrassed in urging others on to fighting, whether they were whole regiments or individuals. We cannot prevent emotion in our hearts, when we read

in his correspondence how happy he feels when
some of his friends are, or will be, out of danger,
while he was never careful of his own life. In the
letters to his wife he very often complains of the
sorrowfulness of his life in being separated from his
home; but never in these intimate letters does he
show any care for his personal safety, or satisfaction at being out of the range of the enemy's fire.
Sometimes he writes before battle as if his only
care were for others.

The second positive point of Schwarzenberg's
humanity was his anxious care for the condition of
the army with which he was entrusted. Nothing
was more painful for him during the expeditions
than the fear that his soldiers would suffer hunger,
cold, and other privations. In the letters from
the Russian war he complains bitterly of the
trouble with the arrangements for provisions for
the army.[1] Once he says that these troubles
and other afflictions could drive him mad. When
in 1812 it began to freeze very early and the
army had no winter quarters, his letters show
his desperate state of mind. Thus he says on
December 4th:—"God grant us Peace as soon as
possible, or it will cause the annihilation of my
whole army, which I could not bear, being so near
the goal. Thus I am never quiet and I feel
terribly uneasy lest in spite of all precautions

---

[1] See the Marshal's letter of July 14th to his wife, and especially
that of August 1st, 1812.

it will not end well." When he finally succeeded in giving his tired army a rest, in supplying the soldiers with new clothes, and in appeasing their hunger, he writes joyfully to his wife :—" In a word, the men look as if they had been born again, and it gives me pleasure to look at them. May I only be able to keep in safety the brave troops entrusted to me, which Providence has so marvellously protected." [1]

The same humanity with which Marshal Schwarzenberg treated his army was shown to all other people. He not only took care of his troops, but he did not allow them to molest and injure the inhabitants, nor to devastate the country through which they passed. Woe to the man under his command who committed such crimes! He hated nothing more than plundering. With great aversion he describes how the Westphalian regiments often committed such excesses. Where they had marched through there was not to be seen a window or door unbroken, nor a trace of flour, nor a living person in the houses. He says that none went so far in plundering as these men. The Saxons were unfortunately known for plundering too, and the Marshal thinks the reason for this was that quite different punishments than those inflicted on them would have suited their national character. Referring to the brutality of the North

[1] The Marshal's letter to his wife from Pultusk, January 20th, 1813.

Germans towards the inhabitants he sees no
other remedy than capital punishment and the
discharge of officers ; yet shooting the culprits
had no great effect upon the others. He did
not himself approve the capital punishment of
soldiers for breach or neglect of duty, blunders in
drilling, etc., but against such excesses he thought
it the only radical remedy. Therefore he did not
agree to the suspension of corporal punishments
in these cases also, as had been done in the North
German States. Murdering, devastation, robbery,
ravishing, were things of common occurrence ; but
what did these wonderfully practical philanthro-
pists trouble about that ? His own philanthropy
had not the power to make him indifferent to all
the misery which stared him in the face on all
sides. His heart aches when he thinks of those
monsters, who, being Germans and soldiers, caused
these two glorious names to be cursed by the
unhappy nations. On this occasion he says it
gave him great pleasure to see chickens and geese
running about in the places through which his
troops were marching, as if they were at home
in his native country.[1]

In 1816, when he was in Italy, he wondered to
see so many poor people, and the words of the
following letter written from Verona to his wife,
on March 21st, show his deep and broad love of
humanity. He says :—" The number of old men,

[1] See the Marshal's letters to his wife, of July 21st–23rd, 1812.

women and children famished and contorted by hunger and misery that I saw at Genoa, Piacenza, and Venice is beyond all human imagination. I confess that on no account should I care to live in a place where humanity in the shape of such horrible pictures of misery met me continually with their lamentations and reproaches for not distributing all my goods amongst the poor."

Another trait of character conspicuously prominent in the portrait of Field-Marshal Schwarzenberg is the deep sense of duty which marked his every step. His duty he understands as towards the State and as a soldier—his duty to the State to which he belonged and to its representative, the Emperor, and his duty to the class or rank of which he was a member. One cannot doubt but that his military education exercised the strongest influence on the development of these qualities. This characteristic is sharply reflected against the very subtle colouring of the background afforded us by the tender relations of the Marshal to his wife and his longing for the happiness of home. His sense of duty and his love to wife and family often contend together in the touching life of our hero and both stand forth in right proportion, provided that we observe them at the same time.

The relationship of Prince Schwarzenberg to his wife is best revealed in his correspondence. That the letters written to his bride overflow with ardent feelings nobody can wonder at, who looks into the dreamy eyes of the beautiful portrait of the Princess by Angelica Kaufmann; but that the last letters written to his wife should abound in the same tenderness and deepness of feelings, is a phenomenon, I think, not often met with.

The most tender outpouring of feelings we find in the letters of the last year's correspondence of the Marshal with his wife; and the concise but apt and striking words of the letter of the 29th of May, 1814, are one of the very many proofs of this. He writes: " You certainly do not doubt how violently my heart beats when I think of our meeting." In the assurances of the Prince to his wife in one of his last letters that he " thinks aloud with her", as he puts it, and that nothing is unknown to her that is known to him, we have one of the numerous proofs of how sincere was the tie that bound together these two souls through the whole length of their life's journey.

This love to his wife the Marshal extended to his family. " My happiness, my bliss is not in the world; at home with you and the children, at Orlík—that is my world, my life." So he writes in the letter from Osjat, August 18th, 1812, while engaged in the Russian campaign. His ideal was neither the glory of war, nor the splendour of the Court, nor the life and bustle of the capital. All his longings carried him continually into the circle of his family. To live unfettered and independent, to belong only to his wife and to his children, to manage his property and to tend and cultivate his lands—this was the picture of life which he had painted to himself and which would have corresponded with his ideas of happiness.

These were the dreams about happiness which seemed to Prince Schwarzenberg most beautiful of all when the contrast between them and the reality was greatest, and when duty most pitilessly called on him to renounce that which was dearest to him. At first, storm raged within, and it seemed that the man would triumph over the soldier. Who knows if, in times of peace, his heart, in these struggles, might not have conquered ? But times of difficulty had come, the Empire was on the brink of ruin, and determined heads and manly arms were needed. No wonder, then, that, in such a great crisis, out of the depths of the Schwarzenberg nature duty came forth as victor. His chivalrous spirit could not bear to leave the flag in danger !

The very first days of his happiness were soon clouded over. The fifth week after his wedding had scarcely passed, his " divine Annie ", whose love had been his talisman on his previous campaign, had only just become his wife, when the sound of the bugle called him into the new fight with France. The first letters written to his wife, after his departure for the field, betray a spirit of despair.

" Oh, my own Annie, what a separation !

Gather all the strength of which you are capable in order to battle with your feelings ; oh, how I realise what a task I am giving you." They are the words of consolation which he sends to his wife from St Hippolit, the first halting-place on his way to the war, March 10th, 1799. For the first time in his life he experienced in his soul the cruel struggle between love and duty.

" How I am fighting with myself! " he writes three days later from Munich. " I must employ all my powers to control myself." At that time, he did not guess how often he would be condemned to repeat these words during his lifetime. Some days after this he was analysing the pains of his wounded heart in his letter from Wolkertshausen on the 8th of April. " Often," he says, " my inward conflict is horrible. To take a battery by storm is child's play to the battle which my head must fight with my heart, so filled with inexpress-ible love for you. Deep in the essence of our beings lies the proof of our union, which in its nature is the closest, the most holy, the most inseparable, which Divine and human laws are capable of forming—and what am I doing here ? "

The answer to this question was given by the battles of Ostrach and Stockach. The feeling of duty conquered, but the conflict between the head and a heart so antagonistic to warfare lasted on. For the immediate future this crisis was partially solved by the courageous determination of the Princess to undertake a journey into the neighbourhood of the enemy's position. This determination operated on the heart of the Prince as balsam on a wound. The hope of the coming of his young wife, in the month of May, was a relief to him in all the privations of the winter campaign. "When frozen to the marrow and drenched through with this cold rain, I say to myself, the month of May will be all the more beautiful, my little Annie will have good roads and beautiful weather and will be able to travel agreeably—and immediately, my own Annie, I feel neither rain nor frost." So he writes from Blomberg on the 12th of April, 1799.

Soon after this, we observe a short interval in the correspondence. They were happy moments indeed, though spent in the vicinity of the hostile camp-fires. The parting, which was obliged to come, was even more cruel. The Prince says of himself " my soul is enshrouded in deep grief ", and his internal conflicts began again. In addition, annoyances arose in the service -- intrigues and cross-purposes in the General Staff —so that in his letter of the 17th of September from Wiebling the Prince conceived the idea of shaking himself free from these disagreeable fetters, and he says : " If I could get out of this complication with honour, I would gladly re- linquish all that I have attained."

This gloomy mood continued, and in the letter

from Mannheim, dated the 28th of September, we read :—" If I have ever wished for anything ardently, then it is, that at the end of the war all others might be rewarded except myself. How heartily I would thank them for this disgrace, which would give me an excuse to extract myself out of these coils." To this depression of spirits was added a bodily illness, which forced the Prince to return to his home in October 1799, where his wife awaited him with his first-born son.

Before a year had expired the same situation was repeated—another painful separation and departure of the Prince to the front, and another visit of the young wife to the seat of war. The letters from the campaign of 1800 again give us an opportunity of observing a further development in his mental conflicts. The crisis of the last year had cleared up a little, and in its place we see a reconciliation : " Teach me to combine duties with duties. A lad of mere reckless courage is not worthy of my Annie ; it behoves your happy husband to stand at the post to which fate has directed him, with steadfast courage and effective strength that animates others. My duty is getting burdensome to me; it is a sour piece of work, without confidence in my troops and without confidence in the leadership of the whole, indeed quite against my own conviction, to be obliged, nevertheless, to act with earnestness and strength."

These words were written on the 28th of November at Ganghofen, five days before the battle of Hohenlinden, and this battle shows how seriously they were meant. The troops under the Marshal were the only part of the army that quitted the field with honour; and that they were not taken prisoners, and were able to retreat with their guns, was due solely to the firm bravery of their commander. The terrible demoralisation of the retreat from Hohenlinden filled the soul of Schwarzenberg with sad thoughts. The contrast between the happiness of home, and the misery surrounding him, was too great not to find the fullest expression in his letters to his wife. The discords which had sounded from his soul in the previous year were heard again. Several times he repeats that the days lived without his wife were lost days. A letter from Burghaus dated December the 11th, 1800, gives us an insight into the very foundations of his nature :—" To live without you, Annie, is for me not to live, still more, it is to suffer.—DUTY! Thou Word of Iron! Never have I felt thy crushing weight more painful! Who can solve for me the great question, what is duty, and how are these duties, which consist in such various, different considerations, related to each other? Here all is gray, dark, and confused before my eyes. My heart, of course, my heart of love, would utter deliverance for me; and yet, in the depth of my being, sounds a voice which simply demands from me the contrary, and this voice I know quite well. It is the same voice that warns me, when my heart is often about to give way, and my head to act thoughtlessly." And this second voice conquered. Undertaking the command of the rear-guard, Schwarzenberg devoted all his strength to the rehabilitation of the enfeebled and demoralised army, and to rescue it from ruin.

Once more, in the midst of the general catastrophe, his soul was shaken with doubts, as is proved by his letter of the 23rd of December from Haag. "What are the duties of a member of society? Shall I, then, thirsting, always see the full cup before my eyes, and never put it to my lips? Have I, then, only become acquainted with the highest height of human happiness, in order to feel the privation the more bitterly? If that is my duty, which I am now doing, then Heaven will provide for me a rich reward—for the self-sacrifice is immeasurable; but if that is not so, if I am chasing some deceptive phantom, Annie, let me cling to you, for I am terrified at this thought. What! Are all these bitter sacrifices to vanish only as smoke? Surely not. When, in the evening, I throw myself on my camp-bed and look at the wretched work done, a voice says to me after all, You have done well, Charles; and I think of you, Annie, and fall asleep,

N

as after a good deed done." Thus, after a new inner fight, came a new victory.

After the peace of Lunéville followed a few years of tranquillity, and these were the happiest of Prince Schwarzenberg's life. But even in these years of peace his duty did not permit him to devote himself entirely to the happiness of his family. The journey to Petersburg in 1801 separated him from his home for a long time, as did also the military demonstration against Bavaria in 1803. Then, when the war with France in 1805, and the ambassadorial journey to Petersburg in 1809, tore him again from his family, his letters sound very melancholy. Thus he writes from Petersburg, May the 1st, 1809, after the outbreak of new hostilities with France :— " My tender, affectionate companion, how I pity you ; how much you have suffered already, my true comrade, worthy of all my love, since your life has been identified with mine, and what you will still suffer ; but I tell you, and repeat it, there will come beautiful days again, and we shall know how to enjoy them." Even in later years all the thoughts of Prince Schwarzenberg are focussed on two centres—the one his duty, the other his love to his wife and family. He had arrived already at an agreement of the two, and both were for him a source of strength and consolation in all the difficult situations of life imposed on him by the State and his profession.

The hope that, after having done his duty, he would be fully recompensed by the glowing happiness of the family fireside, acted upon him like a charm when he felt himself sinking under the weight of duty. In the letter of the 1st of December, 1813, he says beautifully:— " Read in my heart, my darling, you will find there two words deeply engraved—Annie: Duty. Only the thought of you, my all, cheers my whole being, only the constraint to fulfil my duty enables me to find rest and cheerfulness in my inward conviction."

How strong was the support of his wife's love is testified by a few words from the time of the feverish suspense before the fate of the whole of Europe was decided in 1813. He wrote from Melnik on the 16th of August:—"I fall asleep thinking of you. That is so blissful, so strengthening; for you, my darling, will never leave me, even if I stand alone in the world, will you ? " Six days before the battle of Leipzig, the Prince was comforted by similar thoughts:—"My dear Annie, my consolation, the abyss which surrounds me is horrible. If I am dashed into it, you will certainly receive me, and then I shall not need to be pitied; for my soul is clear, and so that which for others might be misfortune, for me perhaps is happiness."

On the 12th of March, 1814, when Schwarzenberg had not received news of the result of the battle between Napoleon and Blücher at Laon, and he

was filled with anxiety as to the fate of the
Prussian troops, having probably in his mind
the recent disasters, he writes from Troyes to his
wife in these words :—" In such moments I take
refuge in you, my darling Annie. The thought of
you cheers my soul ; supported by the conviction
of duty fulfilled, I see only you, and what surrounds
you : the whole world vanishes from before my
eyes. Had I not this consolation, really, I could
at times become mad." The correspondence of
Schwarzenberg with his wife shows indeed with
what difficulty the voice of duty succeeded in gaining the victory over his longings after family life.
What he considered the greatest happiness, he
enjoyed comparatively little ; he was obliged to
sacrifice it, and follow where duty called him.

Not in vain did our hero repeat to himself the
words—" Duty, thou Word of Iron." Thirsting
all his life, he saw the full cup before his eyes, yet
rarely was he privileged to put it to his lips. And
after years of self-sacrifice and anxiety, he was
not spared, even in the very vicinity of the Court,
bitterness and ingratitude. He complains bitterly
on this account in his letters from Milan in the year
1816. From the heroes of the Court camarilla,
the Adjutants of the Emperor, Kučera and Duka,
who found the offices of the Staff a more agreeable
resort than the field, he was obliged to bear the
humiliation of criticism and instruction in military
affairs—he, the soldier and commander, who had

grown up in the midst of the army itself; he, who had taken part in so many campaigns, and spent untold nights at camp-fires, who had shared with his soldiers all sorts of dangers and miseries; he, to whom, finally, all Europe had entrusted its forces, to lead them against the greatest genius of war the world has perhaps ever seen. This censorship was quite in conformity with the disposition of the Emperor Francis, who could not bear strong characters about him, but rather filled his immediate surroundings with servile creatures. But to Marshal Schwarzenberg, who clung to the person of the Emperor with a patriarchal devotion, these rebuffs were a horrible disappointment. There remained for him only the consciousness that he had done his duty, and the hope that he would find some recompense in the happiness of his family at his Orlík. Mentally he had already sketched out a beautiful future in perspective, when he would quit Vienna and the edifice of the Imperial Military Council, with its sombre, malodorous staircases, and remove to Orlík. The winter he would spend at Prague, where he would devote himself to his family and his affairs. But even this hope remained nothing more than a beautiful dream. When he had accomplished the work of his life, and might have rested and enjoyed the days of which he had dreamed throughout its course—" The beautiful days will come again," he had said—then came sickness and death, at an early age, the tragic ending of so many conflicts between duty and happiness.

Princess Mary Annie Schwarzenberg influenced also the other features of the character of her husband. In this union two different worlds met. The Prince received his education at a time when Austrian boys were trained in the spirit of the *Aufklärung* of the age of Joseph the Second, and this was not without influence on the sensitive soul of Schwarzenberg. This is noticeable (as we have pointed out elsewhere) from the way in which he writes on heaven and hell—" If there is a Heaven or a Hell," etc. A man who was a firm believer would not have written thus, and we find in his letters little expression of opinion on religion and supernatural thing'. In the letter of the 21st of October, 1812, from the Russian campaign, the Prince says :—" I can well understand how religious people find, at every opportunity, refuge in their religion : my worship goes out to you. Thence I expect comfort ! You may implore it from Heaven ; and in the blissful hours when we shall rejoice at being once more united, you, my dearest, shall teach me it." Thus the Princess is his mediatress with God, and his instructress in religion. That is a very valuable admission for the comprehension of his religious feelings, and for his whole further development. Princess Schwarzenberg was entirely possessed by the spirit of German Romanticism. The world of

religious emotion stood open before her, and her whole being was saturated with mysticism. And she seems to have opened this world to her husband. He calls her, in his letter of the 27th of October, 1812, the " Priestess in the Temple of his Happiness." Unfortunately we have only one-sided information concerning this relationship, namely, from the reflections found in his letters ; for the Princess, who survived long after her husband, burnt all her letters before her death, except one which she wrote on receipt of the news of the victory at Leipzig. But a number of extracts from the Marshal's letters show that it was she who first caused his bent to religion. The great influence which his wife had on his spiritual life is acknowledged by the Marshal himself ; and he confesses that he always felt the need of attuning his soul to hers, and of thinking and feeling in harmony with her, and he asks if this is not what one calls the harmony of souls. At another time he says of himself, without any hypocrisy :—
" Formerly I was a libertine by choice ; now I am a severe moralist through love." We often find in his letters, especially before decisive battles, the request to the Princess to pray to her God for victory. A month before the battle of Leipzig he wrote :—" Trusting in your God, I do not lose heart, and I am working." Similarly, he wrote in a letter from the first war after his marriage, on the 15th of September, 1799 :—" Thanks to

the Fates, or to God, whom I shall soon learn to love, because you love Him." It appears to have been the world-wide events of the years 1812-14 that achieved the revolution in the soul of the Marshal. In his correspondence at the time of the convulsion of Europe, he often writes of his confidence in God. Not long before the battle of Leipzig the Marshal, in the letter to his wife of the 11th of October, 1813, strengthened himself with this prayer :—" May the All-righteous God strengthen me, that I am not overcome : so I pray, so must Annie pray with me. May the Eternal God bless my righteous undertaking! Amen."

In the night, some hours before the fate of Europe was decided at Leipzig, when "the thunder of the cannon announced the importance of the day", the Prince closes his letter with these words :—" Now, my Annie, I will think of you, and will lift up my eyes to Heaven, and entreat God's protection, and there my prayer will be united to yours." After the war also the Prince ascribed the success achieved to the help of God. " At your feet, my Annie, I lay the sacred laurels that God the Almighty has granted me. God has blessed our arms, the defeat of the enemy is un- exampled. . . . Annie, I have dealt honestly and truly, I have waited patiently, and Heaven has blessed me." Several similar extracts could be made from these years ; in the end, Marshal

Schwarzenberg came to consider himself an instrument of the Providence of God. " I do not fail to recognise the blessing of Heaven that rests on my head. I was chosen an instrument of God—and therefore I trust in His protection."

In his relation to Nature, as in that to God, the chief influence was that of his wife ; and it showed itself, quite in the spirit of Romanticism, in the Rousseau cottage in the Orlík park, where they might listen to the mysteries of Nature. The dreamy love of his wife for flowers and trees was imparted to her husband. Not even the horrors of war could repress this love of Nature in the Prince. In a letter of the 19th of August, 1812, from the Russian war, he writes to his wife :—" In the meantime take care of Orlík for me, my little one. Prepare the seat where I rest, tell me all about the park, about all the paths, and all the spots that are so dear to you, for that is enough to make them unforgettable to me, and you know that there is no tree, no corner that is unknown to me ; when I am on the march and at other seasons, when I have time to think about myself, those are my favourite dreams, I accompany you on the various promenades, there we exchange remarks, propose improvements, discover new views and discuss the execution of many a plan." This was written while Schwarzenberg was pursuing the army of General Tormasov over the desert marshlands of Upper Pripet.

Whoever observes the great influence which
the Princess exercised on the Marshal may ask
himself, perhaps, whether her opinions did not
also influence him in political and military matters.
The letters of the Princess herself might have given
us a sufficient answer, but she unfortunately
burnt them before her death.   With such an
unusual commingling of soul in both husband
and wife, such an influence is very probable.
Even in the Marshal's letters passages can be
found which seem to bear testimony of this.
When at the commencement of the year 1813 of
all the great army of Napoleon there remained
only the troops of Schwarzenberg, and only he
was capable of opposing the Russian advance,
the question was whether Warsaw should be
surrendered to the Russians or whether the
Marshal should resist them.   When the letter
came from his wife to which he replied on the
27th of January, 1813, the Prince wavered.   He
wrote as follows :—Ah, Annie, you say to me
so beautifully, so significantly : ' Oh, do not
fight ! '   It does me so much good to be able to
say to myself, Annie would be content with me,
if she knew how much I suffer, how much I risk,
in order to act according to my conviction."
And further in the same letter :—"Be calm, Annie:
if blood should be spilt, it will not be on my head ;
for I have neglected nothing, in order to stave off
this disaster."   We will not maintain that the

Princess's letter decided the Marshal to relinquish Warsaw to the Russians, and retire without fighting; but at least it confirmed him in this intention. Another proof that the Princess, in her letters to her husband, touched also on matters of politics, occurs at the time when peace was being concluded with France in 1814. In the letter of the Marshal from Bar-sur-Aube on the 3rd of February, we read :—" In any case, my dear Annie, it is certainly time to conclude the peace, for I am in favour of the old French frontiers, and, *as you say so justly*, of a Regency ; but how to attain it, that is the question." Perhaps we should learn more respecting the influence of this gifted lady on the development of events, if her correspondence had not become a prey to the fire.

If we were called upon to state what further trait in the character of Marshal Schwarzenberg is, in our opinion, the most striking, we should not hesitate to point to his wonderful modesty, his absolute contempt for glory. We read with astonishment with what sentiments he accepted the news that he was about to attain the highest possible distinction in his profession, namely, his promotion to Field-Marshal. This was in the Russian War, and was due to the suggestion of Napoleon himself, to whom he had just sent his Adjutant, Count Paar. The Prince wrote about it to his wife in a letter from Koszar on the 31st of August, 1812, in the following characteristic words :—" Napoleon told Paar that he had demanded of the Emperor the dignity of Field-Marshal for me, and that is calamitous ; I am not at all worthy of it. My inner satisfaction is my reward; the confidence and respect of my comrades in the war, that is my pride. The rank of Field-Marshal is inconvenient at this moment, it affords me no pleasure, and will stir up a swarm of envious riff-raff—but now it will be impossible to avoid it."

In all his dealings, he was led only by an endeavour to reach the goal set before him and the fulfilment of his duty. The accomplishment of the purpose sufficed him, he never acted from ambitious considerations. How little popularity and glory pleased him, is well shown by the words written, after the victorious battles with Tormasov in Russia in 1812, about which much had recently been written in the Vienna newspapers : " Unhappy are the people who think that bliss depends upon how often they are mentioned in the public journals."

When the situation in Russia began to be desperate, he expresses his satisfaction to his wife in a letter of the 21st of October, 1812, as follows :— " I must preserve the honour of the Army, and keep it from an unequal fight and from being ignominiously scattered. That is my duty, which I shall solemnly carry out, and then, if Heaven should grant me such good fortune, I shall retire from the scene very calmly, and trouble little about the hissing or clapping."

Another utterance from the depths of his soul we read in the letter written during the operations of the following year, 20th August, 1813, at Laun, before the march of the Bohemian army into Saxony, and to Dresden :—" God knows I have a gigantic work to accomplish: my courage increases in proportion to the difficulty. If I am defeated, it is not my fault, for I am free from thirst after honour, and enter on my great work with all the strength of my soul." In the second letter of the same day he writes concerning this enterprise :—" My manœuvre is very daring, and if it does not succeed, everyone will blame and condemn me, but if it succeeds everybody will say he has advised it—both of which trouble me little —I think only of the purpose." When the operations at Dresden proved unsuccessful, the Marshal complains in his letter to his wife, on the 5th of September, 1813, that at Dresden they failed to advance when he had ordered it, and that the assault on the town did not take place on the day he had fixed, but on the following day. At that time, the Prince continues, " I would have resigned my position, if I had served for glory and not for a high purpose, not for my native country." These personal qualities of Schwarzenberg, this complete subordination of himself to the aim set before him, this complete suppression of personal ambi-

tion, are among the most important causes which
made the co-operation of so many heterogeneous
elements possible, which united European armies
composed of various nations, led by generals of
various qualities, in the presence of three monarchs,
in so gigantic an enterprise, the purpose of which
was the definite overthrow of Napoleon. Any other
commander, in such circumstances, would very probably have destroyed at the outset the harmony
among those engaged by haughtiness and want
of tact, before any decisive action could have been
accomplished; but this harmony Schwarzenberg
preserved, though with difficulty, chiefly by entire
self-effacement.   When in France, in the February
of 1814, Marshal Schwarzenberg did not accept the
battle offered him by Napoleon at Troyes, and
became on this account the object of attack from
all sides, he defended his retreat by pointing out
that the hope of victory was not great, and that in
the end defeat would have destroyed all the previous success, and he adds :—" I can bear it well
enough, that journalists, members of the *Tugend-
bund* and all the rest of them, shout out as loud as
they can : ' Ah, if only some other general had been
at the head of these splendid forces, what grand
things would not have been accomplished ! '—but I
could not have quietly enjoyed with you at Orlík all
the good things that Heaven had prepared for us, if
my conscience were saying to me : ' You had not
the courage to despise the judgment of the world,

you did not act according to your conviction, and therefore a magnificent army has been scattered to the winds, for the triumph of France.' ''

His contempt for glory went so far that he did not even trouble when others plucked for themselves leaves from his laurels. After the victorious conclusion of the War of Liberation and the march of the Allies to Paris in 1814, the Russians were jealous of the Austrians and of Schwarzenberg ; but he commented on their behaviour in the following words :—" As might have been anticipated, it mortifies the Russians, now that they no longer need help, that, after they had been beaten at Lützen and Bautzen, an Austrian, favoured by Heaven, after many victories has brought them here. Now they try with all their might to minimise my merits ; their vain, weak, but cunning Emperor would like now to step out from behind the scenes and receive ovations as Commander-in-Chief. I see these manœuvres increase day by day, but I shall, of course, do nothing against them ; my inner conviction satisfies me richly, and my whole being is occupied with you, my Annie. I am longing for the happiness of my home, there is my life—away from here, back to you, that is my burning desire."

It is no wonder that advantage was taken of this quality of the Marshal, even during his lifetime, that parasites appeared who supported themselves on his merits and that his deeds soon began to be forgotten. This has been the fate of many a great man who has been too proud to take pains about his own recognition. That up to this day there may be observed endeavours to manipulate the light and shade, so that the merit of others may appear in a brighter light, to the disadvantage of Schwarzenberg, is only the result of his under-valuing of fame ; it is true his great soul would bear this injustice calmly, for with him, from first to last, the cause was all. His self-effacement went so far, that he willingly sacrificed his own personal success if he saw that it served to advance the cause. This may be noticed especially in two instances : in the battle of Kulm near Teplitz, against Vandamme, on the 30th of September, 1813, and in the battle of La Rothière, near Brienne, against Napoleon, on the 1st of February, 1814. A comparison of the two battles is very instructive as to the characteristics of Schwarzenberg. In both cases the Marshal, who was distinguished for his reserve and caution in the judgment of a situation, hoped confidently in the success of his arms; yet, both at Kulm and at La Rothière, he gave up the command to others—and just to those who needed it most. At Kulm it was Barclay de Tolly, and at La Rothière, Blücher: both had just been discouraged by previous failure, both were in such a situation that new laurels could restore to them self-reliance and confidence. Schwarzenberg could in both cases reckon that he would win their gratitude and that thus the co-operation of the allied armies would be strengthened, which would benefit the general cause. And this, not personal glory, was his great concern ; the glory he could leave, with almost incomprehensible self-sacrifice, to others. Of course, those who know his character, who know that his heart was not set on this world, can enter into the inner life of his soul and can judge the greatness of his action at Kulm and La Rothière ; nor will they ascribe to his chivalrous spirit the cowardly intention of wishing to extricate himself from a hazardous situation by throwing the responsibility on others.

Together with this trait in Schwarzenberg's character is joined another, not less notable. He not only laid little value on the judgment of the world at large, and had no longing whatever after the halo of glory and the recognition of society ; indeed, he even avoided the great world. This surprises us, in the general and diplomatist as well as in the cavalier. The bustle of capitals was disagreeable to him, their festivities bored him, the pomp of the Court and its atmosphere were often insufferable for him, and he avoided the assemblies of high society whenever it was possible. When he arrived at Petersburg in 1801, the first impression that this great city made on him was one of sadness. At Petersburg he realised fully the hospitality of Russian society,

o

and he noted with thankfulness the consideration and kindness with which he was everywhere met, by the Russian aristocracy as well as by the Court itself; yet he could not overcome his aversion to fashionable drawing-rooms, and he confessed that this mode of life was exceptionally repugnant to him.

Neither did Paris and its society make a more favourable impression on him. The very commencement of his activity as Ambassador at the Court of Napoleon was disagreeable to him. He describes with humour his first audience with Napoleon, how a grand Master of Ceremonies ushered him through chambers filled with people of the Court, how, after the announcement of the arrival of the High Ambassador, two sides of the folding-doors of the reception-room of the Emperor were opened, where he caught sight of him, in the midst of the great dignitaries and courtiers of the Empire. Contrary to his expectation, he is said to have got through the audience very well, but he would rather have undertaken a smart cavalry charge than repeat this comedy. Paris did not in the least allure him by its life, although he acknowledged that one could enjoy oneself there for a few months, but, of course, not as a diplomatist.

This evasion of the rush of social life is a phenomenon difficult to explain in a cavalier accustomed to drawing-rooms from his childhood, in a diplomatist who had moved so much in the surroundings of the Court. But, perhaps, just because his position forced him into the bustle of society, it was most welcome to him to be able to flee from it into the solitude of Nature, and to devote himself to his thoughts and his dreams. Or is there in this something of a Rousseau-like flight from civilised society into Nature ? For Rousseau was not missing in the library of the Marshal, and the Queen of Orlík was Rousseau's especial admirer.

It would certainly be unjust to explain this side of the Marshal's character as misanthropy ; we have seen the very opposite of it in the humanity and the love for mankind which, as already mentioned, distinguished him. He only fled from the splendour and bustle of society and from the brilliance of the Court ; but in the circle of his chosen friends he had a full sense of freedom. As he knew how to love his wife and his family, so he also knew how to share with his friends—not numerous, it is true — the rich treasures of his heart. Those who were most attached to his heart were his comrades in almost every campaign, Princes Maurice and Louis Lichtenstein. Common privations and dangers served only to forge the chains of friendship all the stronger, and to bind together these kindred souls with tighter bonds than the monotonous course of a tranquil life could have supplied.

A very touching picture of the general impression made by the character of the Marshal and his way of dealing with those whom he met is given by the Marshal's biographer, Count Prokesch-Osten, from his own experience. He is said to have spoken clearly, definitely, and with animation; he knew how to convince others easily and was very seldom violent in expression; when, however, this happened, he quickly modified what he had said. He was free from a tone of command, and yet he effected the submission of others by combining firmness with tenderness. He is said to have had an unusual charm and power of attaching people to himself, and even those who envied him and who were his opponents were softened in his presence; his appearance commanded the respect of everyone. He had an unusually acute judgment of people and was able very accurately to estimate their value or worthlessness; at the same time he had the rare virtue of being able to esteem others as they deserved, and was free from arrogance, which tramples on the merits of others. He much valued those who had intelligence, and active genius made a great impression on him, but he could not bear conceit or flattery. He had the power of divining the thoughts of others, and no one who had intercourse with him was beneath his kindness and consideration. He knew how to ease the conversation of all who spoke with him, and he even overlooked awkwardnesses of form if the matter was right. The foundations of his character, severe justice and a mild, kind exterior, were reflected in his features, but temporary impressions never revealed themselves there. His equanimity was never disturbed by moods; he knew how to control his expressions, yet he was not stereotyped, for he had the rare gift of being able to move freely within definite lines. The power of attraction which permeated his whole being captivated not only the cultured, but also the unpolished; but his refined manners could stop any obtrusiveness, while his presence produced an invigorating impression. Besides his exceptional love for his own family, he had great affection for his brothers and sisters, and anyone who saw him in the circle of his dear ones would have thought he was in his proper place, till he was seen under other circumstances, when one was filled with the same impression of him. This characteristic of the Marshal, pointed out by Prokesch-Osten, is in full accord with what one can learn from a perusal of his correspondence. To those who have penetrated, at least to a small extent, into the depths of his soul-life many things have perhaps become more intelligible in Schwarzenberg as a soldier.

Schwarzenberg as a soldier is a problem not easy of solution. We do not see in him one straight line of development, his innermost thoughts and feelings are continually tossed about in the struggles

on which we have touched ; at the period of his
highest development it was no longer his feelings
but the calmest and coolest reflection which compelled him to follow his military course, even
against the impulses of his heart, and to lay all his
faculties on the altar of his native country. And
even to this assertion an exception must be made.
In Prince Schwarzenberg we must make a distinction between the cavalry officer and the general.
At the head of his horsemen, he was quite another
being. It was as if the very scent of the cavalry
squadrons worked on him with irresistible strength,
as if the chords of his inmost being reverberated to
the echo of chivalrous battles of bygone centuries.
There is, without doubt, a trace of atavism in this.
As he led a charge of his troopers, amid the intoxi-
cating throng and clatter of horses and men, and
the glitter of sabres, there was for him only one
watchword—cut your way through ! Whether it
was in the first war against France, in the year
1793, when he surprised the Frenchmen with his
Uhlans at Estreux, or a year later at Le Cateau,
where in a daring attack of cuirassiers he routed
the whole left wing of the enemy, or in 1800 at
the battle of Hohenlinden, where, with his cavalry
regiments, he threw himself upon the foe, in order
to cover the retreat of his infantry and artillery
—in all these and other actions as a cavalry officer
Schwarzenberg gave proofs of his abounding
energy, rapid and decisive action, and unusual

courage. In the retreat from Hohenlinden, when the enemy had blocked the road against the cavalry of the rear at Kremsmünster, it was impossible for their commander to deliberate : therefore to make a dash for it, and cut their way through the infantry of the enemy, was but the work of a few moments. In the war of 1805 we have another surprise cavalry attack of Schwarzenberg in the battle of Jungingen. And what shall we say of the wild ride of the cavalry squadrons in the sortie from the besieged city of Ulm with Archduke Ferdinand, or of the energetic attack in the retreat from Wagram ? And let us recollect how, once more, at Leipzig, when on the 16th of October the situation was becoming critical for the Allies, the Marshal could not resist rushing into the thick of the action himself, at the head of a regiment of Russian Cossacks.

How can the qualities which we have just described be made compatible with reproaches of hesitation and indecision ? It was certainly a different set of reasons which caused the Marshal to act differently from the commander of cavalry. In the leadership of an army the principal thing is calmness ; there is no place for the fever of cavalry attacks, in which primitive instincts prevail. And this tranquillity never forsakes Schwarzenberg as commander of the forces. His first biographer, Prokesch-Osten, observes with admiration in the Marshal not only his clear view of things and his moderation, but also the calmness and greatness which characterise an experienced warrior.[1]

In calm consideration another element of his soul-life comes into operation. In our earlier reflections on the character of the Marshal we have seen that the fundamental principles which guided all his actions were consciousness of duty and humanity. His scrupulous conscientiousness and his love for mankind remain in the field the guiding stars of his actions. His realisation of duty commands him to fulfil conscientiously the task imposed upon him, and his humanity orders him thereby to take the greatest care of the precious human material entrusted to him. He knew how to join both duties. He did not improvise battles as he did cavalry attacks ; he calculated with the greatest prudence his own strength and that of the enemy. He reckoned with all possible eventualities and always covered well his line of retreat ; by manœuvring he endeavoured to force the enemy into an unfavourable position ; he waited until he had all his available fighting forces in a definite position, and then he began to fight, after having guaranteed the greatest probability of victory. With him a battle is not a purpose, but only the means to a purpose, and his purpose is always the destruction of the enemy, and thereby the attainment of peace. Never longing for the

[1] Prokesch-Osten, p. 335.

laurels of warfare, he never rushed into any un-considered and aimless battles ; his dislike of unnecessary shedding of blood withstood such a course of action. In this respect he is the very opposite of Czar Alexander. An Austerlitz is impossible in the history of Marshal Schwarzen-berg; we know also that at Austerlitz his advice was against giving battle and he wished to wait for the arrival of more troops, which might have given the campaign of 1805 a quite different result.

His conscientious and careful preparations for the battle are very well seen in his victories over Tormasov at Pardubitz in the year 1812. In a letter of the 18th of August to his wife, three days before the battle, he says that his manœuvres have already prepared a defeat for the enemy. And in fact Schwarzenberg, leaving only a small portion of his army against the front of the enemy, circumvented the Russian left wing by a large circuitous movement, and thus drove Tormasov to an unfavourable encounter, with a reversed front against a preponderating force, which the Marshal secured by the concentration of all his own forces on the critical spot. Tormasov was indeed defeated only through this excellent man-œuvre. This was quite according to the spirit of Schwarzenberg—the victory was complete and the losses were comparatively small.

Let us turn to the battle of Leipzig. There

we see again how the preparations were made with prudent manœuvring so as to avoid a premature conflict with Napoleon's chief forces, and how Marshal Schwarzenberg decided to strike with all his strength where it was most unfavourable for the enemy.   The first plan of the battle especially, which was drawn up by him, aimed directly at Napoleon's lines of communication, and proposed to circumvent his position entirely, while it compelled him to give battle with reversed front.   We call attention to this slight analogy, although the numbers engaged were different.   We cannot here enter into the difficult question as to what part Marshal Schwarzenberg had in designing the plans of the battle of Leipzig, and what share belongs to his Chief of the Staff, Radetzky; but it is probable that, in addition to a critical consideration of all the plans of operations against Napoleon from the beginning of the war of 1813, a comparison of the battles of Schwarzenberg with each other would throw some light on the matter.   It is, however, certain that the striking prudence of the plan, and the care taken that, so far as possible, all the forces should be focussed at one critical spot, as well as the avoidance of all premature action, entirely coincide with the character of Marshal Schwarzenberg.

The most terrible thought to him was the fear lest the army entrusted to his command should be scattered to the winds and destroyed; and in his letters to his wife, both in the Russian war and in that of 1813-1814, we find deep traces of this solicitude. Therefore he was always most anxious for the preservation of his own lines of communication, as he often affirms in his letters to his wife. This cautious manœuvring, reminiscent of the old school of the eighteenth century, has, however, not brought Marshal Schwarzenberg much recognition, especially from German historians ; he has been condemned, not only for want of energy but also for his reluctance to engage in battles. Only lately has he received some recognition from this quarter, as a strategist. Delbrück, the best authority in Germany on the history of warfare, has in a recent lecture at Dresden fully appraised the strategical faculties of Schwarzenberg. Rudolf Friedrich, in his work *Die Befreiungskriege*, although he is considerably prejudiced against Marshal Schwarzenberg, maintains that, reviewing the long, and as he says, brilliant list of generals of the Allies, perhaps only Schwarzenberg can be considered as a commander-in-chief. He is said to have been, according to the words of the Czar Alexander, "l'homme de la coalition." Of course, Friedrich recognises the personal qualities of Marshal Schwarzenberg, his diplomatic tact in the presence of monarchs, his kindness and modesty, and his capacity for reconciling and conciliating opponents : but his talents for the task of commander-in-chief, in campaigns, he considers insufficient.

We cannot here enter into controversy with him on this point, and we willingly leave it to Delbrück. But one thing we cannot pass over in silence. Friedrich, who is an enemy of cautious manœuvring and a great admirer of Napoleon's violent attacks and his inner line, must himself acknowledge that, in leading the gigantic masses of troops in the year 1813, these tactics of Napoleon were not crowned with success. With an army numbering 200,000, Napoleon had all the strings in his own hands; he could command, and, being a master of the inner line, he knew how, by force of his tactics, speedily to subdue the enemy. It was quite otherwise with an army numbering half a million. In that case the base of operations had so greatly extended that single corps and armies, sent against the foe from the inner line, manœuvring over so wide a territory, became totally cut off from Napoleon's control. The marshals of Napoleon, who were accustomed implicitly to obey his commands, were unable at great distances to receive new and final instructions, and, fearing to act independently, had no idea what to do; and thus in the whole campaign of 1813-1814 they allowed themselves to be defeated everywhere, thus ruining the results achieved by the main forces.

Friedrich considers this,[1] together with the bad provisioning, as well as the insufficient means of

---

[1] Rud. Friedrich, *Die Befreiungskriege*, ii. 52-53 : Berlin, 1912.

transport, and the great distance from France, as one of the chief causes of Napoleon's defeat. Marshal Schwarzenberg is reproached by Friedrich with not being a great personality who would have nipped in the bud the least opposition on the part of his subordinate leaders.[1]

First of all, it was impossible for anyone on the side of the allies to act in so imperious a manner, with three monarchs present and asserting their authority, especially Czar Alexander ; and secondly, it was just the way in which Marshal Schwarzenberg dealt with those under him in command that gave the guarantee of success. Marshal Schwarzenberg not only did not cripple the activity of his subordinate commanders, but, on the contrary, as far as the unity of the plan of action allowed, he gave them a free hand and independence. I remind the reader only of the two cases mentioned, when in his presence he gave up the leadership to two commanders under him. The result of this course was that the leaders of subordinate armies and of detachments knew what to do in situations when it was not possible, on account of the long distances, to obtain instructions from the centre : they knew how to act independently and how to overcome the marshals of Napoleon, who were actually hypno-tised by the gigantic personal predominance of their master and were thus paralysed in their

[1] Friedrich, *l.c.* p. 53.

actions when they should have been able to act for themselves. It was as if Marshal Schwarzenberg had anticipated the best way of pushing forward such a host of troops—which, as Friedrich well says, was at that time, without telegraph and railway, an anachronism. They were armies which in their immensity were only suitable to modern times, with all the technical possibilities of to-day. The war carried on by them entirely resembled modern warfare, carried out as it is by enormous masses of troops, divided into a succession of armies, covering an immense territory. This anachronism annihilated Napoleon, but was accomplished, on the part of the Allies, precisely through the fortunate character and tact of Marshal Schwarzenberg, and his superhuman self-denial. To attain the great purpose at any price, even at the price of his own person, to preserve unity and that even by sacrificing himself —these alone were the great objects he had in view. What in Marshal Schwarzenberg's action has been ascribed to weakness, was often the only possible course, if the unity of the Allies was not to be destroyed.

That he was conscious of the enormous task put upon him by his position, at the head of the allied armies in the War of Liberation, and that he should have relieved his oppressed heart in his letters to his wife, is really not to be wondered at. Only an utterly thoughtless and superficial character, devoid of conscience, could without lines of care on his brow have undertaken such a task, unequalled in the history of Europe. But what he laments most is not the difficulty of the task, but the presence of the monarchs, and chiefly of the Czar Alexander, and his continual interference in the operations. And from this there was no escape. The war concerned the most vital interests of all the monarchs, and they would not have been pleased to be sent home by anyone's orders. There was nothing to be done but remain commander and diplomatist at the same time. And old Blücher honestly bore witness to these complaints of Marshal Schwarzenberg, by his well-known remark that Schwarzenberg had defeated Napoleon in spite of the presence of three monarchs. Nor can the course of events in France in 1814 be ascribed to want of energy on the part of Marshal Schwarzenberg. There the operations were often so dependent on diplomacy, that often the most incomprehensible strategical movements are only to be explained by political causes.

During his long military career Prince Schwarzenberg gave many proofs of unusual energy. The discipline of the army he always considered as the cement, with which all was held together; and when the most difficult but most brilliant task of his life was entrusted to him, was it possible that his energy should suddenly have failed him and his sense of discipline have been lost ? What psychological explanation can his critics give of that ? I think the best reply to them will be the words of the greatest contemporary English warrior, Wellington, who said of Schwarzenberg :—" He was a great general, and withal so good and mild."[1]

[1] Kerchnave-Veltzé, *Feldm. Fürst Schwarzenberg*, p. 147: Vienna, 1913.

A DEFENCE OF MILITARY HISTORY

SYNOPSIS OF PAPER READ

BY PROFESSOR C. W. C. OMAN

A SCHOOL of modern historians has systematically depreciated the study of military history. As a fair example of their view take J. R. Green's *History of the English People* (preface).

" It is the reproach of historians that they have too often turned history into a mere history of the butchery of men by their fellow-men. But war plays a small part in the real story of European nations, and in that of England its part is smaller than in any. The only war which has profoundly affected English Society and English Government is the Hundred Years' War with France (1336-1451)."

Apparently then neither the campaign of Hastings, nor those of Plassey and Quebec, nor the War of American Independence, nor the Napoleonic War, played any great part in the development of British institutions or social and commercial conditions !

This strange view is due to political and personal bias. The old school of historians imagined that the main trend of the annals of the world was determined by great personalities like Alexander, Julius Caesar, Mahomet, or Napoleon. The modern liberal teacher of history wishes to substitute the view that " the people " must always be the protagonist. The " hero " of the type that Carlyle praised must be turned into a mere typical development of the tendencies of his age and race, whose greatness shall not offend the susceptibilities of smaller minds, or sin against the great doctrine of equality.

Moreover, wars are disliked by teachers of this school, because they wish to look upon all history as " evolutionary," while wars are often " cataclysmic "—the intervention of the abnormal and the unforeseeable often breaks the even flow of development. The " cataclysm " is usually caused by the appearance of some individual with unusual powers and endowments. Writers of the evolutionist school try to get rid of this fact by declaring that these outstanding individuals are merely the necessary outcome of their surroundings, *e.g.* Sir John Seeley once wrote that if Bonaparte had not been Bonaparte, Moreau would have been ! As if all military dictators would have been the same in their workings. Would Moreau have assumed the crown of Charlemagne, or carried his army to Berlin, Vienna, and Madrid, if he (and not Bonaparte) had overthrown the Directory ? This is to ignore the fact that

Bonaparte by his special combination of world-wide ambition, military genius, and organising power was an utterly abnormal personality—which Moreau certainly was not. So with Mahomet—to say that the success of the religious movement which he started was merely due to the weakness at a certain epoch of the Roman and Persian Empires, which gave him a unique opportunity, is to ignore the fact that both Rome and Persia had been weak before, and that prophets had often arisen in earlier times, whose teaching had no such consequences. It is personality which counts, much more than environment.

To take the most obvious instance from English history. William the Norman determined the whole trend of our mediaeval annals by his military ability. If the campaign of Hastings had gone otherwise than it actually did, we cannot doubt that the history of the next three centuries would have been very different. Granted all that historians (set on justifying the *fait accompli*) write about Saxon England being ripe for conquest because of its want of a strong executive and a good organisation, it is yet clear that no other conqueror arose beyond the seas with the strength and ability of Duke William in those ages. Normandy and her neighbours never produced another such commanding figure. Without him and his military ability England would have worked out her fate on other lines—for good or evil.

Much the same may be said of the work of
Alexander the Great ; it is the unique personality
which is more important than the unique opportunity in the working out of the history of the world.
Opportunities arise in scores—they only become
important when the individual who can utilise
them arises.

Many, if not most, of the governing figures of
history have been military. It is absurd to argue
that their methods of war do not form an important
item in history. To ignore them, or hand them
over to the military specialist, is unworthy of the
self-respecting historian. Nor must we neglect
other methods of war, not united with a single
great name like Alexander, Hannibal, or Napoleon,
but perfected by schools of leaders like those who
built up the Roman legion, the tactics of the
Turkish light-horse, those of the English archery
of the thirteenth to fifteenth centuries, or the
Swiss pikemen. All these purely military facts
had grave influence on whole centuries of political
and social history.

A general knowledge of the outlines of military
history, therefore, is as important as that of social,
economic, or political history. It should be as
discreditable to an educated man—much more
to a statesman or generally one of the governing
classes—to be ignorant of what military facts
governed the event of the day at Hastings,
Salamanca, or Trafalgar, as to confess that he

knew nothing of the Reform Bill of 1832, the Home Rule crisis of 1885-6, or the Parliament Bill of 1911. Military history must have its share in every well-considered educational curriculum.

FOREIGN REGIMENTS IN THE BRITISH SERVICE, 1793–1815

SYNOPSIS OF PAPER READ

BY C. T. ATKINSON

WELLINGTON's army in the Peninsula included a non-British element, the King's German Legion and other regiments. In this it was not different from the armies of the day, the enlistment of foreigners being practised by all nations; and Great Britain was actually distinguished from other countries by prohibiting the custom in peace, though utilising foreigners extensively in war to make up for the weakness of the normal establishment.

Three types of foreign troops in British employment may be distinguished : subsidised allies, *e.g.* the Prussians in 1794, paid by Great Britain but not directly controlled ; troops belonging to other countries (*e.g.* Hesse-Cassel) hired by Britain and under British control but not part of the Army ; regiments which were raised for King George III.'s service and which formed part of the Army.

Of these the first were the least satisfactory,

and the second were but little used after the Peace of Basle (1795) had neutralised North Germany. Most of the foreigners in our service belonged to the third class. These were obtained from various sources ; at first French *émigrés* were available in large numbers, later on prisoners of war and deserters were enlisted. Some corps were raised directly in Switzerland (*e.g.* de Watteville's Regiment), and a few in Germany and Holland. The character of these corps varied greatly, some (*e.g.* the Queen's Germans, later known as the 97th, which did very well in Egypt in 1801) being really excellent corps. By the end of the Revolutionary period of the war the number of foreign regiments had been much diminished, many having died out in the West Indies or being drafted to the 60th Foot, itself mainly a foreign corps.

After the Peace of Amiens only a few corps survived, but on the renewal of war these were much increased and many new ones added. Deserters and captured prisoners were the chief sources from which they were raised and recruited ; and new conquests (*e.g.* the Ionian Islands and the Île de Bourbon) were followed by the addition of new regiments. Greeks and Italians were raised owing to the British occupation of Sicily, 1806-1814. These foreign regiments were mainly employed in the Mediterranean and the West Indies, but the Chasseurs Britanniques were in the Peninsula from 1810 till the end of the war.

A distinction is to be drawn between " foreign " regiments properly so-called and " miscellaneous " regiments, also described as " Colonial " or " provincial." Some of the " miscellaneous " regiments were really penal battalions, quartered in West Africa and the West Indies, and mainly British, though including a proportion of foreigners. Colonial corps included the West Indian Regiments, Ceylon troops, Canadian Fencibles and others. The Brunswick Hussars and Brunswick Oels Light Infantry need special mention, owing to the adventurous start of their career as the Black Legion with which the Duke of Brunswick tried to raise North Germany in 1809. After escaping from Germany in British ships they passed into British service and were in the Peninsula, the infantry serving with Wellington's main army, the Hussars being employed on the east coast.

Towards the end of the war the quality of recruits available deteriorated greatly, and the foreign regiments proved less satisfactory ; even the good ones found it hard to keep up their quality.

The King's German Legion are the most important and interesting of all these troops, but may be considered as in a class apart ; they served George III. as their sovereign, but as Elector of

Hanover, not as King. They are also differ-
entiated by their history having been most
adequately written. La Haye Sainte is also a
constant testimony to their achievements at
Waterloo.

INDEX

Q

PRINTED BY
TURNBULL AND SPEARS,
EDINBURGH

For EU product safety concerns, contact us at Calle de José Abascal, 56–1°,
28003 Madrid, Spain or eugpsr@cambridge.org.